CORNELIUS MINOR

WE GOT THIS.

Equity, Access, and the Quest to Be Who Our Students Need Us to Be

Foreword by Kwame Alexander

HEINEMANN
PORTSMOUTH, NH

Heinemann
145 Maplewood Ave
Portsmouth, NH 03801
www.heinemann.com

Offices and agents throughout the world

> *The author has dedicated a great deal of time and effort to writing the content of this book, and his written expression is protected by copyright law. We respectfully ask that you do not adapt, reuse, or copy anything on third-party (whether for-profit or not-for-profit) lesson-sharing websites. As always, we're happy to answer any questions you may have.*
>
> **—Heinemann Publishers**

Cataloging-in-Publication Data is on file at the Library of Congress.
ISBN: 978-0-325-09814-2

Editor: Holly Kim Price
Production: Vicki Kasabian
Cover portrait and chapter opener illustrations: Jamal Igle
Interior and cover designs: Monica Ann Crigler
All figure art, logos, and backgrounds: Monica Ann Crigler (with help from Getty Images/iStock)
Typesetter: Kim Arney
Manufacturing: Steve Bernier

Printed in the United States of America on acid-free paper
     9 10   VP   24 23 22 21
June 2021 Printing

For Edna Zoe Freeman, who taught a nation, and for Hawa and Cornelius, who crossed an ocean with those teachings, and for Zoe and Kass and Tino and Matti and Soleil and Indi and Xander. May you continue to be all that the ancestors dreamed that you would be.

Contents

Foreword

"The teacher is of course an artist, but being an artist does not mean that he or she can make the profile, can shape the students. What the educator does in teaching is to make it possible for the students to become themselves."

—Paulo Freire

THE FIRST TIME I HEARD CORNELIUS MINOR SPEAK WAS three years ago in a dimly lit room at the International Literacy Association (ILA) annual convention. In the wake of the July 6, 2016, killing by a police officer, of Philando Castile, a thirty-two-year-old black American, ILA courageously programmed a last-minute literacy and social justice–themed breakout session. Cornelius was the co-presenter. The mood around the conference, around the country, was dark. It was all blues. But where there's some love, there's always some hope, and when I happened upon the remote room where Cornelius was spreading his love of literacy as empowerment and action, as a tool for social justice in the classroom, I could hardly get in the room, let alone find a space to sit on the floor.

He stood in front of the standing-room-only crowd of educators and concerned human beings poetically, patiently, and powerfully grappling with classroom equity, privilege, and prejudice—all deep and explosive issues.

His cadence was comforting. His confidence was assuring. And his un-yielding compassion was addictive. If this were a living room concert, he was most definitely the crooner and the trumpet. For sure, America is dark sometimes, but the blues is also about the healing spirit. And Cornelius brought the light.

We all sat listening and learning, not only being charged to resist the way things have been done, to disrupt the status quo, but we were guided toward a sustainable change, and more importantly we were armed with accessible tools and strategies. I'd never heard of Cornelius Minor before that afternoon, but in that room, in that moment, I sat spellbound, cap-tivated, and captured by his vision and leadership, by his pedagogy and activism. As he says, "Change is participatory," and I, like everyone else, embraced his revolution, our revolution: to teach "young people to create opportunity for themselves, *and* teach them to do that work responsibly," and to expect "miracles six periods a day."

This primer supports teachers who want to get on the floor and dance to the beat of classroom equity and access. It's for educators who want to move from culturally responsive theory to practice. It's really a chance to sit in the room with a voice that vibrates with hope and humanity. Like Paulo Freire, Cornelius believes deeply that the social conditions of chil-dren should not limit their education access and opportunity. He knows that communities must be empowered to battle society's constraints and pressures, and this book, with its timely questions and thoughtful an-swers, with its storytelling and strategies, is a weapon for combat. *We Got This.* is meaningful and compassionate literacy. So, come on in the room. Grab a spot on the floor. And let this book be your new jam.

Kwame Alexander
Newbery Medal winner for *The Crossover*
Author of *The Write Thing: How Kwame Alexander
Engages Students in Writing (and You Can Too!)*;
Rebound; *Solo*; *The Playbook*; and *Booked*

Acknowledgments

IN *THE SOCIOLOGY OF ART*, ARNOLD HAUSER SAYS THAT "every artist expresses himself in the language of his predecessors" (2011, 30).[1] In this, I am no different. There are so many people who have made this work possible—who have made me possible.

When I express love, it is because the Minors, the Crocketts, and the Johnsons taught me how to be it. Mommy, Daddy, Zoe, Kass, Soleil, Indira, and Swami, you all are everything.

When I express creativity, it is because the children of New York City challenged me to embody it. Much love to every young person at MS 331 in the Bronx and to each kid at the Brooklyn School for Global Studies. You encountered a young dreamer and you would not let me rest until I became an active doer. Thanks to my colleagues. You all made me. Ainate Yiaueki, every lesson that I teach carries your fingerprint. I will always be your coteacher. The PTA mothers at Global, you all kept me alive. You read me books and made me eat sensibly and tolerated my skateboarding and demanded that I never stop striving to be the educator that the children needed me to be. Everything that you all did for me . . . it mattered. It still does.

---

1. Hauser, Arnold. 2011. *The Sociology of Art*. Translated by Kenneth J. Northcott. Chicago: University of Chicago Press.

When I express insight, it is because Kathleen Tolan, Lucy Calkins, Mary Ehrenworth, Audra Robb, and the entire team at the Teachers College Reading and Writing Project created the space for me to attain it. You all crafted opportunities for me to teach until I was clear and study until I was certain, and then you taught me to stand in front of others and to be myself. You all opened doors for me, and as I grew, you nudged me to be bold enough to cut my own keys and to eventually open those doors for myself and for others. Thank you. There will be more young educators, like me, who will arrive at your doorstep with heart and potential and unorthodox vision. They will need your ears and your support. I hope that we will always have a home at TCRWP.

When I express bravery, it is because the Bowen United Methodist Church community, the Florida Agricultural and Mechanical University family, and the #EduColor collective made sure that I always exemplified it. Schools, communities, and organizations all over the world have supported my quest to learn and to teach. From Seoul to Seattle to Lawrence to Eagle Butte to Santiago de los Caballeros, there have been kids who inspired, teachers who innovated, and families who believed. Your belief and your time and your efforts have sustained me. Every kid, family, and educator in Trenton, Pacifica, Los Angeles, Shanghai, Alexandria, Chicago, Groton, Houston County, Wethersfield, Singapore . . . I can't possibly name all of you here, but we lived this—together. Thanks.

When I express wisdom, it is because Holly Kim Price, Vicki Boyd, and the entire team at Heinemann forged a path for me to seek it. I can be a mess of a teacher most of the time. Thank you all for seeing me anyway, believing in me, and dragging this book out of me. Patty Adams, Vicki Kasabian, Edie Davis Quinn, Monica Crigler, Eric Chalek, Elizabeth Silvis, Brett Whitmarsh, Lauren Audet, Cheryl Savage, Sam Garon, Michelle Flynn, and the event people, Natalie Pavlov and the home team, all of you have taught me, through your tireless work, that we all have something to say and that it is worth every sacrifice to say it. Thanks for making this happen.

Liberia. ATL. NYC. Forever. ForeverEver.

We are educators. Our realities are not easy ones. At all.

We carry the collective hope of eighteen or twenty-eight or thirty-seven students at a time.

And it is hard for some of our students to hope when there are bullies in the locker room,

when there is never anyone at home,
when there is only food at school,
when the traumas of the world weigh them down in our classrooms,
when their unique abilities or ways of knowing are not acknowledged or respected,
when we don't construct realities that include their two moms or one grandparent or adopted family,
when their gender does not match the restrooms or roles that we force them into,
when there is lead in the water,
when the police kill people that look like them, or when the lobbyists and legislators make it easy for people to buy automatic weapons and walk into classrooms.

It is hard to marshal hope when the world's capacity to care is often directly proportional to the number of digits on their parents' W-2.

But we do it. We do more than hope. We make miracles six periods a day.

In a world marked by histories, doctrines, policies, and beliefs that can sometimes drive us apart, what we do is vital. Mathematics, history, arts, sciences, writing, and reading matter immensely. But these disciplines are not the entirety of our work. They cannot be.

Education is about two things—teaching young people to create opportunity for themselves *and* teaching them to do that work responsibly—with respect to our environment and to the myriad communities of people that share our planet.

Anything that abridges opportunity or compromises our responsibilities to one another is our enemy. As such, if we are not doing equity, then we are not doing education.

This is immense work, but this work of ensuring equity and access is doable. We inherited this calling from our predecessors.

And we move forward armed with tools and with strategies. This book is full of them.

Our journey starts with an understanding that no great good can be done for a people if we do not listen to them first. Powerful teaching is rooted in powerful listening.

Introduction

We All Want Better

THERE WERE A FEW THINGS ABOUT THE UNITED STATES OF America that assaulted my senses almost as soon as I stepped off the plane for the first time—the sun did not shine with the equatorial intensity that I was used to, the sound of English being spoken without the usual Liberian musicality required my ears to do more work, and my parents seemed to become fiercer versions of themselves. Instantly. They trusted nothing, behaving as if everything in this new land could kill me.

The usual reminder "I love you, son," came bundled with stern warnings like "Do not talk to strangers!" and "Stay close to the apartment!" and "Hold my hand!" Though I was too young to understand why, I was able to surmise that to my tough West African parents, all of these things were some version of love.

Love can be strange.

Back then, everything was. I was an elementary school student from Liberia, and I did not understand a lot of what was going on around me. I had so much to learn then. I still do now.

I grew up in a home that my parents fortified—with light, laughter, and love—against the terrifyingly unknown aspects of our new country that were gathering right outside of the apartment door. My parents knew little about hamburgers, comic books, video games, and hip-hop. Much to their confusion, these were the things that became my new nationality.

In our home, the typical preadolescent battles that should have been waged over remembering one's chores were instead fought over the fact that for a time, I abandoned jollof rice for Happy Meals, Anansi for Spider-Man, and highlife for hip-hop.

My parents would not have it.

Each day they would see to it that I ate proper Liberian meals, they would tell me stories until my sides hurt from laughter, and my mother's hi-fi cassette tapes poured Liberian soul into every room of the house.

My mother and father reminded me constantly that I would always be Liberian—that I would always be me. "Stop trying so hard to be them, Cornelius. They are great in their own way. You are great in yours."

As an educator in a system that feels like it can sometimes value compliance over creativity, I remember those words often. We are asked to do a lot in this work. This does not bother me. We are here to do great things.

What concerns me is that given the profound challenges that we face in the classroom, we are most frequently asked to try really hard to be "them."

We are asked to be them when our responses to children are dictated by what the curriculum *allows* as opposed to what kids need. We are asked to be them any time we are asked to adopt a classroom stance that does not honor multiple ways of being, knowing, and communicating. We are asked to be them when we are told to work in ways that are blind to the contexts of family, community, culture, power, and oppression.

As educators, we know that we find much of our power in collaborative work. When our ways of seeing children, planning for them, facilitating opportunities, and reflecting on those experiences are informed by what we learn from each other, all kids benefit.

Being our brilliant, passionate, and creatively flawed selves is hard. We invent things, try them, and make mistakes. Our successes are not overnight, and the work required to get to them can feel imperfect. When we are not being assaulted by our lack of sleep, we are besieged by the guilt, fear, and uncertainty that are often associated with not always having the answer. In loving response to this, there are movements in our profession that seek an alluring kind of uniformity—one that promises to make this work easier by rooting it in a fidelity to mandate that threatens to homogenize us into a collective "them."

Love can be strange.

But, we don't have to be that. We don't have to be them. You, friend, are already great in your own way, and I think that we can be great together.

No matter what drew us to teaching or how we got here, we all have a few things in common.

To start, we all want better.

The paths that we have chosen to actualize *better* are as varied as our expertise, our backgrounds, our communities, and our schools. Still, we, as a profession, are united in the reality that we want better experiences for children and young adults.

We want them to have access to art, music, and movement. We want them to know more science and math and history. We have done everything in our power to create opportunities for them to read well, think critically, and write expressively. I know this.

I also know the world that I see outside my window.

And I'm not OK with it. At all.

I know that the things that we want for children cannot happen optimally if kids attend schools that are underequipped to serve them or their communities.

Growing up, I knew that my ability to make and sustain a life for myself was intimately connected to my teachers' ability to authentically see me—a relative outsider—and to effectively teach me. Many of them excelled at this, but as my friends and I matured, it became clear that schools, no matter what they profess, simply function to perpetuate the inequities already present in the communities that house them.

Some communities have been crippled by poverty or robbed of access to opportunity by de facto segregation and by policy. Others have been rendered silent by selective empathy, complacency, or apathy.

Hard work, creativity, and honesty were the norm in my neighborhood. They are in most places. But the rewards for those things—opportunity, access, social mobility—were often reserved for the rich kids on the other side of our town.

It is probably like this in your town.

I want better. This is why I came to education. I wanted to teach kids how to write well. Beyond that, I wanted to teach them how to spin those words into opportunity, into capital, and into freedom.

I taught for years—first in the Bronx, New York, and then in Brooklyn. During that time, I became obsessed with a question: What does it mean to be appropriately equipped to serve a community and its most precious resource—its children?

That question and the journey that I've been on since asking it drive this book.

My job has changed over the years, but my pursuit remains the same. I am still learning what it means to be appropriately equipped with not just the resources but the content knowledge, the teaching methods, the interpersonal skills, the social consciousness, and the kind of audacious attitude required to serve children powerfully.

Currently, I am a staff developer. I work with teachers in classrooms all over the world.

I have worked with thousands of students and hundreds of teachers across over thirty-five school districts representing countries on five continents, and I know one thing for sure: there is no single answer.

I'm encountering all kinds of things on my journey. I know that our work is curricular. Always. But it is also interpersonal and political. I cannot teach kids to write—or to do math, or art, or history, or coding—with content alone. Education should function to change outcomes for whole communities. And if I'm serious about community building, I've got to invest regularly and wholly in the people, the relationships, and the mechanisms that form the community. It takes time and serious imagination to learn to do that.

In this book we get to do that. Together.

I always thought that when I sat to write the intro to my own book, somehow this would mean that I had made it.

Though I've come a long way from sneaking ninety-nine-cent cheeseburgers into my parents' house, I don't have the sense of relief that I thought I would have at this point in my career.

Stepping off the plane over thirty years ago, I was just learning to see people, things, and experiences that were different from me. Eighteen years ago, I was just learning how to really see an entire classroom. I was teaching myself to see each child in it, to see each kid's talents and personal aspirations, and to see the hopes handed to the students by their communities. This was beautiful work made complicated when I was also forced to regard and participate in the scholastic, institutional, and social mechanisms that kill opportunity for so many students.

My career has been defined by my attempt to bridge the enormous gulf between the promises of education and the actual lived experiences of so many of my students. We, as a profession, have been forced to surf the tension between what should be and what is.

Now, I don't see just my classroom. Because of my work with children and teachers, I get to see into classrooms across town and over oceans. Because I have actually shared classrooms, lesson plans, failures, and triumphs with many of your fellow teachers, I know what you have come to know, and I know that you feel this tension too.

I am still ill at ease with the world. My senses are still under assault from some of the things that we experience.

This is a strange feeling that imposes a particularly uneasy consciousness. Most days I move through the world wearing a complicated smile. I love my students, my colleagues, and my work. But I don't love the reality that for all we know about thinking and learning, we have not turned our knowing into universally equitable access to opportunity for all of the students that we serve.

I am not OK with a world where only some people—the ones who were born on the right side of town or the ones who happened to make the right friends—get a shot at success.

You aren't either.

As teachers, we cannot guarantee outcomes—that all kids will start businesses, lead their families, and contribute in their communities—but we can guarantee access. We can ensure that everyone gets a shot.

Consider this a manual for how to begin that brilliantly messy work. We got this.

PART 1

This Ain't Everybody's Hero Story— It's Yours

My first understanding of a superhero's origin came from a hand-me-down Spider-Man book that my cousin let me borrow. He handed it to me in Sunday school. The cover was so inviting that I excused myself to the bathroom—eschewing a lesson about Paul in Damascus to hide out beside the urinals and read about Peter in Queens.

Sister Jones, my Sunday school teacher, was one of the church mothers. She wore only white and smelled like peppermint. She gave out the best candies after church and birthday cards with crisp five-dollar bills annually, but none of this obscured the terrifying fact that she was quick, she missed nothing, and she was not afraid to punish another person's child.

So with my book hidden in my ill-fitting suit jacket, I slinked toward the bathroom, knowing that I would not have much time to live in Peter Parker's New York. Once there, I read quickly, voraciously. I did not savor the words and images. Time and fear of Sister Jones would not allow this. Even so, I knew that this book was powerful. I could not wait to talk to my cousin.

When I got to him, I recounted the hero's story in the kind of reverent detail that Sister Jones reserved for hymns and testimony.

"He was bitten by a spider and became very strong," I started, exhaling the words as forcefully as I had taken them in moments before. "Then something bad happened, and he did not use his powers to stop it," I continued. "He felt guilty and resolved to always help people. Then he did. And no one could stop him." I paused.

"He knows . . . that with great power comes great responsibility." I exhaled a final awestruck, "Wow!" That mantra left my heart racing. In many ways, it still does.

I have come to learn that every generation has its hero story, and each story has its accompanying mantra. The contexts of those stories are different, but be they real or fictitious, when we tell the stories of our heroes, they all have the same arc.

Our heroes are created from a simple template. Even when they do not fit cleanly, our retellings and mythologies make them fit.

They are usually incredibly powerful and chosen in a fatefully divine moment. They confront the things that are clearly bad—no gray areas—and they often do this work alone. They suffer few setbacks, but when they do, they are didactic ones. Their good intentions and their sacrifice downplay or mute any collateral damage.

And they all end with a similarly themed mantra.

Great power. Great responsibility.

Do your best. Never quit. Treat people fairly. Stand for what's right. Truth. Justice. National pride.

All of these can be beautiful statements of ideal, but the thing about hero stories and mantras is that we, as a society, believe them. Wholeheartedly and to a fault.

When one considers Western civilization, the hero ideal—more than religion and capitalism—is our national and economic ideology. To varying degrees we subscribe to the myths that there are people who are somehow better than us, who possess an uncannily elevated ability to focus, to work, to think, and to act, and that these people's extraordinary abilities mean that they are more worthy of moral authority and economic prosperity.

When we talk about ourselves, these are the stories that we tell. This is our mythology and our popularized history.

This is Gilgamesh, Ulysses, and Zeus. This is George Washington, Alexander Hamilton, and Ragged Dick. These are, of course, the fictions we consume. This is Batman, Wonder Woman, and Spider-Man. Even when we seek to make that narrative more inclusive, we end up telling the same story.

One person. Incredible will. Divine ability. On a mission to save us all.

This is Susan B. Anthony, Martin Luther King Jr., and César Chávez.

These are the athletes we cheer for. These are the leaders that we want to elect. These are the people who we hope will teach our children. We want them all to have hero-like qualities.

The problem with this narrative is not those people. They are brilliant. The problem with this narrative is that it erases the complicated calculus of becoming and being a hero, a leader, a change agent, a teacher. This narrative does not allow heroes to be imperfect or to be nuanced. It does not allow them to grow tired, to fail, to learn publicly, or to grieve. As such, it is exclusive.

> *"He knows . . . that with great power, comes great responsibility."*

Any narrative that mutes or denies imperfection silences and refuses our essential humanity.

The subtext of all of this says, "You can't quite be a hero, because you are tired, and heroes don't get tired, and because you are confused or angry or unready or broken." We have been taught that none of these things is heroic. And to some extent, we have believed this—both text and subtext.

Stories are a powerful blueprint for what is possible. The histories that we choose to tell regulate our imagination for the futures that we aspire to build. That these stories often get told in a way where Elizabeth Cady Stanton, Bayard Rustin, and Dolores Huerta don't exist as easily as their contemporaries limits how we understand, plan for, and work toward change.

We can learn lots from hero stories, but sometimes they leave out the concrete realities of change.

> Though **change** is personal, this kind of **work** requires a team of people who will not (and should not) always agree with you. Often, you'll have to deal, in some public way, with your own flaws.

> **Change** is participatory. There is no program you can buy or person you can pay to make things better for you.

> **Change** is not a one-size-fits-all thing. Nor is there a single solution or panacea for real progress. The **work** that is required feels like trial and error (and error and error) most of the time.

> Working toward **change** almost always means that we must abandon ways of doing things and thinking things that are not working. One cannot change outcomes for a student, a classroom, a school, or a district without changing one's own behavior and thinking. In this, sometimes we fail or undermine our own **work**. We can forgive ourselves for this and continue moving forward.

> This **work** is not instant. There is no quick path to success. Things won't always go well the first (or second or ninth) time. We are allowed to fail, reflect, improve, and **try again**. This is the only way.

The "teacher as superhero" story can be similarly misleading.

We cannot begin to fully understand this story without a quick examination of why people would construct such a narrative in the first place. To consider Batman as a hero, one must acknowledge Gotham City, its inhabitants, and their storied mythology. He does not exist without context.

To consider teachers as heroes, one must acknowledge schools, communities, students, and the uneasy history that binds them. We do not exist without context either.

"Any narrative that mutes or denies imperfection silences and refuses our essential humanity."

The inhabitants of Gotham live in fear of evident crime from a few public crime lords. In his universe, this is how things are for Batman—this is his status quo. Batman knows this. His crusade is not just against the crime lords. His work is fundamentally disruptive because it aims to change the status quo. The only people who oppose him are those who benefit in some way from the way things are.

Schools are economic and political constructs. This is how they are. The leaders in China's Song Dynasty saw them this way and they articulated it clearly. They erected schools as a pathway to civil service jobs. As such, school was at the center of economic stability to the governed and civic stability to those who governed. This, of course, was not without its problems. In theory, all males were eligible, but the cost of an education—even in the year 960—was great, so only the sons of well-off parents could afford to succeed. This meant that only the sons of well-off parents got good jobs. For centuries, few challenged this.

"We are allowed to fail, reflect, improve, and try again."

In the 1770s Thomas Jefferson grappled with this issue. In an ideal sense, he saw schools as a political safeguard from the potential tyranny of a king. In a democracy, white men would vote for those who would govern. But to vote, he contemplated, one needed to understand the issues of the day, and he believed schools could serve in this capacity.

Since Jefferson, educators have sought to raise the quality of education and to broaden access to it. The work of teachers has not been just to teach. For generations, educators have labored to ensure that access to schools (and to the opportunities that schools guarantee) extended equally not just to men or to the wealthy but to all learners. This work is economic, it is political, and it is disruptive; it seeks to change the status quo by making room at the table for all of us.

There are those who oppose this kind of work, and they do so partly because, whether they know it or not, they benefit in some way from the way things are.

So why the teacher-as-hero mythology?

Because if educators are working toward equity, one way to silence them is to deify them.

In both its fact and its many fictions, the story of the superhero teacher creates a set of problematic expectations for our profession, the people engaged in it, and those that we labor to serve.

It suggests that one can work alone, that constant sacrifice is the expected method for doing this work well, or that our work is the result of some kind of inherent or mystical goodness and not years of careful practice and study. It allows one to discredit work that is in progress or those who do this work in nontraditional ways, because heroes can look only like Hilary Swank, Michelle Pfeiffer, Edward James Olmos, Sidney Poitier, or Glenn Ford.

One way to take your voice back is to expand the narrative.

The thing that they rarely show you in the superhero books and movies is the practice montage—the time that people spend getting good. Even in the biographies we read, little attention is given to the time that our real-life heroes spend missing their families, the time they spend second-guessing themselves, disagreeing with their allies, or recovering from the stresses of the job.

I'm a writing teacher. Many of us are. We can help the profession to craft a better hero narrative. In doing so, we can craft better heroes . . . not just for the students that we hope to teach but for the world that we hope to build.

"We can help the profession to craft a better hero narrative. In doing so, we can craft better heroes . . . not just for the students that we hope to teach but for the world that we hope to build."

1

Begin by Listening

"Those are the bad guys! How am I supposed to fight them? With these powers?!"

WHEN I WAS KID I USED TO SKATEBOARD A LOT. I WAS ALWAYS trying some new thing. Probably 25 percent of my life up until my late twenties was spent recovering from being regularly bruised, scraped, and banged up. Growing more proficient at the sport did not mean the end of casual injuries; it simply meant that I consistently found newer, more artful ways to introduce my shoulders, elbows, knees, and backside to the pavement. After years of doing this, pain was no longer a deterrent or threat. It was simply the currency that I paid for the ability to fly.

On this planet, gravity comes for everyone. Except me. I could manipulate physics with wooden boards. Because of this urban alchemy, for a few brief seconds at a time, I was exempt from Newton's laws. To be this, however briefly, is to be free.

There were times when that freedom landed me in urgent care. The doctor would always start by asking, "What part of you hurts?"

Because of my intimate relationship with pain, my answer was almost always, "Everything."

So it is with teaching. At its core, what we do is as necessary as it is poetic as it is soulful as it is liberating. In teaching we are delicately human. Through teaching we can be powerfully immortal. But for many of us, it just hurts. Everything hurts.

When things hurt, it feels logical to look for the person or thing doing the hurting. In hero terms, we need a bad guy or a supervillain.

In education, we have done this. We look to oppressive systems, to testing, to segregationist funding and zoning practices, to ableist notions of what kids can and cannot do. In our worst moments, we blame ourselves or we blame children and their communities.

Though it may feel like it, the supervillain here is not testing or mandates or any of the other things that we often talk about. These are *significant* problems, but they are simply underbosses—the large regional crooks that keep our attention away from disrupting the foundations of the myriad barriers that stymie our progress. The true masterminds—the *real* enemies—in this dystopia are the business-as-usual attitudes, binary thinking, and *inflexibility* with which we have been conditioned to approach these problems. These things have robbed us of our power and of our curiosity. Without them our revolutions die before we can even think to start them.

We live in a world that is cast in ideological counterchange—black or white, whole-class novel or student choice, rule follower or renegade. We don't have to.

Metaphorically, though we all have different needs, we've been handed the same graphic organizer, and few know or even question why we are filling in these boxes.

This impacts teaching because it limits our creativity. In a world of this or that, our very ability to respond to students, their families, and our communities is limited to paths of thinking, speaking, and doing that are prescribed by ideologues who do not know us or the powerful work that we have been called to do.

New teacher. Veteran. Admin. Rural. Suburban. Urban. Even when those words apply to us, they are not all of us. We are so much more than those labels. Each time I accept a label for myself or for my work, I am painting myself in hues that do not fully match my purpose or my unique ability to fulfill it. Each time I allow myself to be defined by a thing, I am implicitly denying the many states of being that are not that thing.

To choose to live out the first few years of my profession as a "new teacher" ignores and silences all the parts of me that are not new to children, to cities, to youth culture, or to literacy. Yes, someone new to the profession has lots to learn about teaching, but that person has skills and knowledge that we would be foolish to ignore. Similarly, to subscribe to the falsehood that my years in the system make me a veteran ignores and silences all the parts of me that still need mentoring and community and new insights and feedback and love.

Those labels cannot cover our whole humanity. Neither can those we apply to students—language learner, special education, gifted. All are problematic. As are those that we apply to society at large—woman or man, rural or urban, poor or wealthy, minority or white.

We lose lots of human capital each year because people bearing essential insights and experiences are wearing labels that we've been conditioned to ignore.

Beyond that, what we name things impacts how we think about them. When we are inflexible in our naming, we become inflexible in our thinking. How often have we been told that "this is the way to reach boys" or that "language learners need this thing." Such talk is a necessary shorthand. It's the parlance of our profession, but this cannot be the entirety of our thinking. We need tools to build a bridge between the discourse of our profession and the children that populate the communities that we serve.

When we are inflexible with our approach to school, kids and their families and communities are unheard. This is one of the great evils of modernity. Whole communities are rendered silent simply because we have refused to hear them.

Inflexibly following mandates, curriculum, or educational fads puts us at odds with or robs us of the ability to see nuance, just as doing things as they have always been done or teaching to the test can prevent us from teaching to the children assembled before us. Under this weight, our students become data points; they lose their personhood. We are a profession that talks about *students* now. We don't talk about *kids* anymore.

The antidote to all of this—our teacher superpower—is not some mythical teacher goodness or hyperbolic self-sacrifice. Those things do not exist. Our superpower is *listening*, and there are several tools, attributes, and strategies that can augment our listening.

The ability to listen will not make teaching easier. It will not take the painful parts away, but listening can give us our children back. If we listen to what children and communities are saying, and we respond accordingly, we can be ourselves again. We can be people. And if we can be people

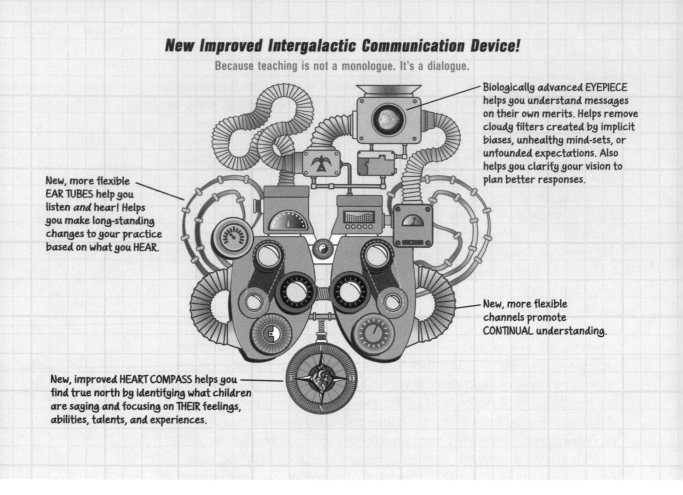

New Improved Intergalactic Communication Device!

Because teaching is not a monologue. It's a dialogue.

Biologically advanced EYEPIECE helps you understand messages on their own merits. Helps remove cloudy filters created by implicit biases, unhealthy mind-sets, or unfounded expectations. Also helps you clarify your vision to plan better responses.

New, more flexible EAR TUBES help you listen *and* hear! Helps you make long-standing changes to your practice based on what you HEAR.

New, more flexible channels promote CONTINUAL understanding.

New, improved HEART COMPASS helps you find true north by identifying what children are saying and focusing on THEIR feelings, abilities, talents, and experiences.

together, we'll discover that people can make things easier. We are all the answer that we will ever need. We always have been.

You can transform your teaching; your team can transform your school; your school can solve real community problems. If you listen.

How Listening Can Help

Brooklyn is poetry. As such, everything that kids bring to our classrooms is symbolic. In this town, craft matters. Details matter. Style matters. When thinking about students everywhere, it's easy to miss that simple understanding: With the kids that we teach and with the work that we do, it is rarely ever about the what. It's about the how. The meaning in this art of teaching lives there—in the style.

Meaning. For children, the same is true of how they exist both in and out of academic spaces—meaning is the panache with which they take a school-issued polo and wear it like a royal tunic. That *means* something.

It's not the words that they utter; it's the reality that kids can make the sweetest words burn like acid or the most profane utterances sound like prayer. That ability to learn, approximate, adapt, repurpose, and re-mix—that *means* something.

The beautiful thing is, most students walk into our classrooms with these skills. That kind of learning-on-the-fly is second nature to anyone who has ever played outside, enjoyed a game, experienced a toy, or lived with a sibling. These skills are transferable. They work outside of school and can work just as effectively inside. This means that we can use that innate improvisational nature to ensure that the learning that they do in the world does not die at the classroom door.

This is how I try to meet all kids. "Where is the poetry in this young person?" With Quick, I did not have to ask. His poetry was immediately apparent, as there is nothing more poetic, nothing more symbolic than the names that we choose or, in his case, the names that choose us.

Quick was appropriately named. He championed talk of his athletic prowess. Any teen would. It gave him tons of social capital. He was revered by his peers, and though his chosen appellation applied equally to his godlike facility with books and numbers, he was not as universally adored by his teachers. Though I didn't really know why, even I kept my distance.

So it shocked me when he asked to hang out during lunch one day. "Minor, what do you do during lunch? Do you hang out with other teachers and stuff? . . . No, wait. That's too many ladies for a guy like you." He smiled.

Though the smile drew me in, I deflected the joke with a well-used line. Kids were always trying to turn the teachers' lounge into a reality show. "Now, Quick, you know that there ain't no—." But Quick was quicker.

"Minor, you know I'm just playing. Actually, I need your help."

"Quick, to my knowledge, you are passing all your classes. You don't need my help," I interrupted. I was still perplexed by Quick's uncharacteristic candor.

In that moment, the playfulness left him. He became immediately distant again. What was buoyant and boyish just seconds before became visibly world-weary. I saw it darken his eyes, and the heaviness rode the timbre of his voice.

He huffed. "That's the problem with you, Minor—all you teachers. You want to make everything about reading or math. It's not always about that, Minor. It's not always about you."

As the words rushed forward, I attempted an apology, but there was no space between Quick's words. He intensified. Each utterance was measured, focused, piercing.

"Minor, I can't go to my house anymore. My mom . . . the bills . . . our landlord changed the lock. The counselors. They all came and assigned me to a shelter. They assigned my sister to a different one. I'm not leaving my sister. I'm not going there. I need you to tell them that I'm not going there. Not without my sister."

"Quick, the counselors, they can help—" was the beginning of my offering.

True to his name, he cut me off again. Fast. "No, they can't. I already told you how they tried to help me. Now I need you to go tell them that I'm not going."

I did not know how to calm him. My attempt at doing so was weak. "But, Quick, I don't know anything about that. I'll talk to them. But I'm sure the counselors have done everything."

"They have done everything except listen to me. Minor, all of y'all want to use your essays and your vocabulary words to save my future, but none of y'all know anything about saving my now."

I was silent. To this day those words still float through my consciousness.

He continued. He was much louder now. His "I'm talking to a teacher" tone had been evaporated by the intense confrontational urgency of his truth. "If you're so good at teaching, teach me how to solve this. You know this neighborhood, Minor. You know what it is. I'm not the only one in this school that needs to learn."

That was a challenge, issued in the way that all urgent challenges are—with no apology.

It has been more than ten years since that exchange, and I'm still trying to become the teacher that Quick needed me to be in that moment. He had no use for the nebulous future of literary essays and Latin word roots that my class seemed to offer him. What he needed were tools—weapons, really. He wanted to learn how to speak. He wanted to learn how to make himself heard.

Quick was not asking me to solve homelessness. He just wanted me to teach him how to use his voice. The failure of my teaching back then mirrors the shortcomings of our teaching in general. My lessons were not, at all, linked to Quick's reality.

Actually, I had taught him how to speak. I had taught him how to be heard, but I had failed to connect the dots. I had failed to show him how our literary essays were arguments and that those arguments could be constructed in a way to get counselors to listen. They could be built to show evidence that might help the director of homeless programs to bend a rule so that it would allow one's family to stay together. One does not have to teach the specifics of homelessness if one is always seeking to understand students and laboring to teach the specifics of transfer. Intelligence does not live just in the essay; it lives in how we apply the skills embedded in essay to everyday life.

"Intelligence does not live just in the essay."

There are many attributes that make someone the kind of person that kids habitually choose to learn from. When personality is fatigued, and warmth dims, or patience subsides, kids will regularly choose to invest in us if we always help them to see that what we are offering will help them to live better—in the future, of course, but most urgently, right now.

The way that we get there is by listening.

How to Listen to What Students Are Really Communicating

As we work our way through this book together, we will come back to this action as an answer to the things that plague us and our work, as a process to work through the multiple professional challenges that we face, and as inspiration to power us through the Atlas-like trauma of carrying worlds of expectations on our shoulders.

Here I posit authentic listening and the actions that result from it as the most radical of all teacher behaviors. When we seek to craft better realities for our students and our peers, our listening has to be informed by what we know, by what we are learning, and by our desire to actually hear what our students, communities, and partners are telling us. This kind of listening has three parts.

1. There is the act of listening itself, more specifically, the hearing. This is the stuff that happens at the actual site of the message being delivered. Sometimes that message is communicated with words that are either spoken or written. Those messages are decently easy for educators like us to receive, but sometimes messages are communicated through behaviors or through silences, and sometimes the messages do not happen in one instance; instead they are communicated across several instances over time.

    However the message comes to us, the role of the educator during the first part of any communicative act is to simply hear. Not to judge, not to solve, not to prescribe, but first to hear. Sometimes it helps here to ask gently clarifying questions to confirm what you've heard or to paraphrase in order to communicate that your partner has been heard. Quick needed me to put my relative ignorance on issues of homelessness to the side and to just hear him. All of my attempts to console or calm him were rooted in my desire to solve his dilemma. Had I really listened, I would have known that he was not seeking solutions. He was seeking *me*. Most of our students don't want complex solutions or programmatic approaches. To many kids, "my teacher hears me" is solution enough.

2. After we hear, we've got a bit of thinking to do. After receiving any message, we've got to name what we think we heard and plan a response. In teaching, responses are not just what we say; they are what we do and the habits and rituals we establish. These things, more than anything else, communicate that we value what the people in our school communities bring to the table. As we engage in this work, it is important to recognize that understanding what others communicate and making sense of those ideas are both value-based actions. Because we spend a lot of time communicating with people who approach school with different values, full understanding might not come readily to us, and that is OK, as long as our work is characterized by active study, so that our understanding deepens with time.

Quick needed me to be the kind of teacher who could teach him how to turn literary tools into implements of social change. I had gotten to literary proficiency, but I had fallen tragically short of showing him how that proficiency could translate into competence at navigating his life. I missed the whole point of school, because I wasn't good enough at listening yet.

3. Most of this book focuses on the question that guides the third part of authentic listening as I present it here. After hearing and thinking, we must ask ourselves, "Because of what I've heard, how can I make active and longstanding adjustments to my classroom community, to my actual teaching, and to how the department, grade, or school operates?"

Here, we recognize that teaching is not monologue. It is dialogue. And after hearing what kids have to say, I've got to *do something*.

Participating in that dialogue requires us to kill the assumption that children and their understanding of the world are flawed without us. We know that quite the opposite is true. We are in this profession because we believe that they have the answers.

Many of us come to this knowing that we teach kids so that they can deal with the challenges they will encounter in their lives, not so they can navigate the challenges that we faced in ours. To really move kids, there has to be some act of continual understanding. There has to be evidence that the teacher is learning from students too.

Understanding why children choose to learn is one of the first things that I can learn from students. Fortunately for us, children choose to learn for the same intrinsic reasons that adults can choose to learn. I choose to learn something because it

- can help me to solve a problem that feels very real to me
- gives me greater freedom in my life as I live it right now
- creates an opportunity for me to do something that I want to do soon
- feels like a worthy challenge—to me
- helps me to do something good for people that I care about
- connects me to people that I want to know

▣ is fun or cool (as I define it)

▣ allows me to survive something or someone that threatens my well-being.

So what do these reasons for learning mean for my teaching every day? Anytime we introduce a lesson or activity, it's important to be clear about why this experience is happening in our classroom.

How to Ensure That Your Lessons Speak to What Students Say They Need

There are concrete ways we might set the stage for learning. I start with some thinking using the questions in Figure 1.1. The first thing I have to do is be clear on the actual skill I want to teach kids, not just the activity that I want them to complete.

Admittedly, kids will never get good at a thing if they do it only once. Each experience has to give kids several opportunities to try a skill. I also want to communicate quite clearly to kids that I am not expecting perfection each time. The desire to get it right often limits their ability to think flexibly and to take risks.

Finally, I want to build a bridge for children—a bridge between what we are doing in class and the lives that they lead outside of class. I want to be able to show kids how each skill I teach in class makes life right now better outside of class.

Much of this has to be presented in a way that kids can understand and value, so I also spend some time thinking about my presentation. The chart in Figure 1.1 gives me a convenient way to plan all of that thinking. (A blank template of Figure 1.1 [Online Resource 1.1] as well as all other Online Resources cited can be accessed at http://hein.pub/wegotthis and by clicking on Companion Resources.)

If I want to engage kids further, I can offer some choice. Using the chart in Figure 1.1, I can prepare a series of lessons for the week and start this way:

> Kids, I've been listening to you this month, and I'm noticing three big things:
>
> 1. A lot of you have been talking about how your parents give you no freedom.

2. Also, ever since that argument went down in the cafeteria, you all have been especially concerned about relationships and friendships.

3. Finally, some of you all have been talking nonstop about the Yankees. I'm trying to figure out a way to get them to notice us. I think that it would be cool if some of the players knew about what we do. . . .

So here's a choice: I can teach you two things this week. How should we focus our learning? We'll be writing essays, but I can use essay work to teach you how to

1. Get more from your parents,

2. Make stronger relationships and friendships, or

3. Reach out to our favorite ballplayers, hopefully in a way where they'll notice us.

All of these approaches make a nod toward what kids value, what they know, and what they hope to master. Also, all of these things advance the literacy goals I have for kids.

There are a few replicable steps to ensure that your lessons speak to what students say they need:

1. Listen to children. Notice when they express interest in a thing. Even if it is not a thing that you understand or care about, it is important, *right now*. You have to accept the reality that over the course of a school year this thing will change, and you'll have to assign importance to something new.

2. Ask sincere, nonjudgmental questions to deepen your understanding of that thing. Kids can tell when your questioning is respectful, when it is dismissive, or when it's patronizing and voyeuristic. Simple utterances like, "Tell me more . . . ," or "Where could I go to learn more about that?" can be revolutionary. Asking, "Is there a kid in this class who is an expert that we could all learn from?" and then doing a little bit of work to follow up on that questioning sends an equally powerful message that you are not the center of this classroom. Kids are.

Figure 1.1 *Lesson Plan Thinking Chart*

What's the activity I want to do?	What skill(s) do I need to teach so they can do this activity?	How many opportunities will this activity give them to practice this particular skill?
Do a thematic reading of a text. Write a quick response to the text.	I want them to be able to consider the larger ideas that make texts work and to comment on those ideas. I can model and teach this.	If they choose their own texts, each kid can try this once and then develop that idea. If they have opportunities to work with partners, they will have access to someone else's thinking too.
I want them to be able to read articles and ask questions about the things they do not understand.	I need to teach them how to look at information, determine what they don't know, and ask a question. I can model and teach this.	Kids can practice this in several articles, maybe as they browse a magazine or a database. Maybe we can watch an informational video together. I can pause every thirty seconds to practice asking questions.
I want kids to write evidence-based essays.	I want to teach them how to evaluate information gained from what they read and choose the most powerful information. I can model and teach this.	Kids can practice this in talk. During read-aloud we can use partners to discuss and weigh evidence.

What might I say so that what I want to teach aligns with what kids want to learn?	How will mastery of this specific skill allow them to live, play, work, exist in ways that are measurably better?
"Reading this way is important and all, but did you know that thinking about themes helps us in our personal relationships too? Understanding theme can help us understand why people do what they do, and this is the kind of understanding that makes people love and respect you more. . . ."	"When you can think and talk about larger issues in books, you can do the same in life. This can help to strengthen relationships and friendships."
"When you read nonfiction, you are not supposed to understand everything about the topic yet. Having questions about the text is cool, and asking questions about the text makes you smarter. Asking questions about things that you see on television or about things that happen in your life makes you seem engaged, and the more engaging you are, the more people want to be around you. . . ."	"When you can ask questions, you learn more because those questions guide your brain to take in more information. In conversations, this communicates interest. People want to engage with you more."
"I know that a lot of you wish that your parents let you have more freedom. I know that this is going to sound funny when I say it, but most parents want you to have fun; they just want reliable information about what you are doing so they know you are safe. Today, when I teach you how to write, we are going to practice adding reliable information. This is going to make you great at writing and great with parents."	"In life, being able to communicate your ideas with strong evidence gets you what you want. It does not work every time, but people are always more willing to consider your point of view."

3. Usually, their interest in a thing fills a social need. Ask yourself, "Why are the kids into this?" Is it simple fun, or is it about belonging to a group? Does that thing help them to navigate something tricky or achieve something cool?

4. Teach with that need in mind by modeling the skill in the academic context and then by showing how the skills acquired in your class transfer—how those skills help them to navigate the challenges in front of them right now.

5. Give them multiple opportunities—through assignments, projects, and conversations—to practice that thing in an academic context and in the context of their own lives. Ideally, those two contexts intersect.

If the option to learn with me is always a mandate enforced by my authority as a teacher, then there will always be children lining up to fight me. If the opportunity to learn with me is a choice that I help students to recognize and make, then in my classroom, they can become free.

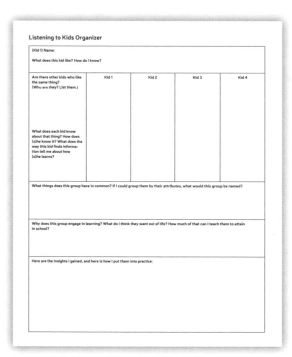

Figure 1.2 *Listening to Kids Organizer*

As such, how we listen and what we do with what we hear matter. Figure 1.2 is a quick mental matrix I use when I'm listening to kids. It advances some of the questions offered earlier. It's a mental matrix, because these are not notes that I compile physically. We've got so much other stuff to keep track of—so much to collect, write, grade, and warehouse. This organizer simply helps me think and plan.

A blank template of the Listening to Kids Organizer (Online Resource 1.2) can be found with the Companion Resources.

Figure 1.3 shows how a tool like this helps me prep for class.

Figure 1.3 *Listening to Kids Organizer Sample*

Listening to Kids Organizer

(Kid 1) Name: Taylor				
What does this kid like? How do I know?	She likes video games because I hear her talking about them all the time. If and when she is off-task, it is almost always about video games.			

Are there other kids who like the same thing? (Who are they? List them.)	Kid 1	Kid 2	Kid 3	Kid 4
Mark Juan Khalid Hoang What does each kid know about that thing? How does (s)he know it? What does the way this kid finds information tell me about how (s)he learns?	Mark Knows what his friends tell him. His learning seems pretty social. I need to create opportunities for him to listen to and talk a lot with peers.	Juan Seems to know a lot; always shares tips with the others. Says he learns from visiting two game blogs that he trusts a lot. He's a researcher, knows how to tell good sources from bad ones.	Khalid Knows all the specifics of the game and about the context of the whole video game industry. He likes to browse game magazines in the library. He does not read text as much as he grazes it. He still manages to learn lots . . . hmm?	Hoang English language learner. I'm not sure what he knows about the game. Though he speaks very little, he follows every conversation about the game. He plays online at night with all the other kids. His ability is more advanced than I give him credit for.

What things does this group have in common? If I could group them by their attributes, what would this group be named?
This is all of the quiet boys and Taylor. I would name them that. Some of my quiet kids like video games! One thing that I'm noticing is that this is not video games generally. This is the game Mario Kart specifically.

Why does this group engage in learning? What do I think they want out of life? How much of that can I teach them to attain in school?
They seem to band together for social reasons. Mark and Hoang are not as into Mario Kart as the others, but they are into the reality of having a group—a crew to belong to. Maybe for this group, angling my teaching to highlight the skills that allow you to make and maintain friendships will be important.

Here are the insights I gained, and here is how I put them into practice:
This is a group that needs to stay together. Conventional teacher wisdom says, "They're all friends; break this group up!" Instead, I want them to understand that the ability to stay productive while hanging out with people that you like is a skill that they will need in high school, college, and the workplace. Synthesis is a thing for this group. I might move them out of longer texts and move them into several short texts at a time about a topic. This group needs time to graze the texts, gather information, discuss, and reread the texts. Reading for them is not linear or solitary. It is social. It is OK for this group to read and think as a collective. I can make space for this, by giving them a quiet corner to huddle together in during independent reading time. For them, this time will not be silent. It will be quiet. I want them to know that difference: that even though they will be talking, they can still be quiet—and productive.

Listening in this way means that you are radically kid-centered, that you are adaptive, and that you are willing to take public risks. Not everyone at school is. Being these things will make you a better teacher, but sometimes being them can make you stand out. Standing for children is the most powerful thing a human can do, but it is never easy.

"Education has done very little to shift power or to distribute it evenly. Rather, it has functioned to ensure that power stays where it has been—among the wealthy, among the men, among the white people."

2

You Can Disrupt the Status Quo in Your Class

"Poverty. Race. Gender. The deck is stacked against many of my students. How can I disrupt the systems that govern my classroom?"

KAL-EL, THE BEING WE KNOW AS SUPERMAN, IS AN ALIEN.

I don't think that enough people consider this reality. He is not human. In almost every iteration of him, despite his incredible power, he is generally ineffective as a hero if he chooses not to engage with the humans among whom he lives. They mistrust and misunderstand him and his motives. To some on Earth, Superman is no hero.

The Man of Steel is most powerful when he chooses to understand humans, when he works alongside them, and when he is guided not by his superior might, but by humanity's vision for itself. Ultimately, when he considers himself a savior, things don't go well for Superman. When he considers himself an ally, reality bends to his will.

We are teachers, and the same is true for us.

But usually we know how to ally only with the agreeable kids—the "good" ones, the ones who are most like us. How do we hear the kids who aren't?

Teaching cannot work optimally if it is not rooted in this kind of community engagement.

We are most powerful when we labor to understand young people and when we work alongside (not for) them. When our vision for kids and for classrooms is guided by a community's vision for their own children, our work becomes real to children and to parents. Relationships are appreciably challenging to maintain, but they become infinitely easier when they are grounded in a shared vision and genuine collaboration.

Teaching without this kind of engagement is not teaching at all. It is colonization.

"Minor," he called to me in his usual Brooklyn parlance. In Red Hook, I was not Mr. Minor. I was simply Minor. Usually this was uttered respectfully. My years in the neighborhood bought me a credibility that my general greenness at teaching did not.

"Minor. I don't . . ." There was something tentative, almost pleading in the way that he continued. I should have known that something was up. Brooklyn kids are never this tentative in public.

"Can't I just stay in here? There's already a lot of people in there and . . . All of us don't have to go to the computer lab, do we?"

"We're all going," I replied in that tone that teachers use when they really mean, "Don't ask me any more questions."

Jeff understood the message, and because he was a good kid, he complied. In my mind, I had won.

As one would expect, in his mind, he had lost. He carried this loss visibly. He sulked.

Jeff was a kid who needed routine. I knew this, but this knowledge evaporated when I learned that the computer lab had twelve seats open for the period. I saw it as an opportunity for the students in my small class to finish their video blogs, and I made the impulse call to study there instead of in our classroom. To Jeff, this thirty-meter trip was a surprise. He knew he did not deal well with surprises. His pleas were an attempt to communicate that.

In the adolescent chaos of that room, Jeff had understood my message, but I had failed to understand his. I hadn't listened.

He was set for failure.

And when it met him, it was swift, powerful, and all-consuming.

Settling into the computer lab was a soap opera of middle school emotions. There were already a few kids there with Mr. David, our no-nonsense school aide. People had their "I always sit here when we come to the lab" seats. Others wanted to be partnered with friends. Some scrambled for the computers with the cool games. Caught in the spontaneity of that opera, Jeff's meltdown started innocuously.

"I can't find a seat."

At that point, I was in full "make it up as you go along" mode. I was determined to make this spontaneous class session work. As such, I could barely read Jeff's situation; all I could do was respond to the words he had spoken to me.

"There's one by the window," I answered without really even regarding him. My head nodded in the direction of a vacant terminal, and my body was already moving toward the sound of student need elsewhere in the room—eager to put out the next fire—completely unaware of the ember I had just sent to smolder by the window.

A hot ember just needs a strong wind. In our school, there was none stronger than Mr. David. I did not witness the catalyzing breeze, but by the time Jeff responded to whatever Mr. David had said to him, it was too late to stop the conflagration.

"Noooo, Mr. David, I'm *not* moving! Minor *told me* to sit here!" I saw him peel away from Mr. David's firm gaze, and he sat—planted himself, really—exactly where Mr. David said he shouldn't.

Mr. David's voice grew in volume and intensity. Conversely, I could see Jeff shrinking, swallowed by the attention from his classmates, Mr. David, and me. He seemed to be losing his purchase on his world. He sobbed audibly and clutched the keyboard in front of him. It shattered in the intensity of the moment. Lettered keys rained down on the floor. They scattered in every direction. They were met there by tears, which were now pouring from my student, Jeff.

Mr. David said something about property damage. In the seconds it took me to understand what was going on, accusations were made and counselors and school security were summoned. I thought about

"This was a small part of a child's soul being crushed."

damage. Kid damage. Jeff damage. At this point, he was as broken as that keyboard.

I was by his side, but when school security arrived, I wasn't. He was handcuffed because it was 2004 and there was "zero tolerance."

"Just . . . ask . . . Minor. I'm supposed to sit . . . there," he heaved between breathless sobs. They escorted him out. I followed wordlessly to the door. His eyes met mine. "Minor . . . Tell him. . . .

"Minor."

Usually this was uttered respectfully. In that moment it sounded vacant and defeated.

I've seen meltdowns before, and this was not that. This was a small part of a child's soul being crushed. I replay this moment often. I've talked through it with friends and mentors. We always try to explain it away. The moment refuses to leave.

I understood Jeff, but I did not act on that understanding. I knew that he did not deal well with surprises. I knew that he needed structure and options and clear instructions. I gave him none of those, because like a misguided Superman, I was acting on my own might. Jeff's vision for himself, though he tried to help me to see it, was invisible to me.

My own tears came then. They were for Jeff, yes. But where were those tears seconds ago? Why didn't their sudden emergence compel me to act then? With Jeff shackled and beyond my reach, those tears were useless to Jeff. They were my selfish catharsis. They were the tears of a colonizer. My future was comfortably certain. His future was unfolding in front of me—black, male, handcuffed, labeled—it had just become a statistical kind of certain. On my watch. In this version of Macbeth, the blood of King Duncan—King Jeff—was on my hands too.

I don't remember signing up to be in an oppressive movement, but there I was standing in wordless, tear-stained consent at the door of the establishment.

There is a current moving through our schools that pushes young men like Jeff out—a nexus of rules, policies, and adult misunderstandings that works like a subconscious heartbeat to push these boys toward prisons. In that moment, I was complicit. We've all been.

When we think of race-, gender-, ability-, or class-based oppression, we often think of individual acts of personal bias. Our minds fill with images of a villainous past—"back when things were bad." We consider Klansmen and burning crosses, or we remember the men who spat at suffragists and the police officers who arrested them for attempting to vote. We use words like *racist* or *sexist* to describe those people as if those words were merely personality types or character flaws.

They are not just character traits. Racism, sexism, ableism, and classism are systems. They are the rules, policies, procedures, practices, and customs that govern a place and lead to consistently unequal outcomes for specific subsets of people.

For example, it has been well documented in American life that a gender pay gap exists. Though some dispute how much it is or exactly how to calculate it, it is known that in most industries, given an equal investment of time, education, effort, skill, and experience, an American woman will make less than an American man. This is an economic reality.

This reality does not exist because there is some nefarious person running the payroll offices in the top businesses. This reality would exist even without ill-intentioned people, because there are systems in place that ensure that such a pay gap persists. Course offerings in schools, career counseling, scholarship availability, professional organizations, internships, and opportunities for mentoring all work in concert, creating more opportunities for boys to advance.

A young woman who attends a school where she is not encouraged to take physics or where there are few opportunities to work with a mentor is disadvantaged before she even enters the workforce.

"Systems don't change just because we identify them; they change because we disrupt them."

The hard part of knowing that oppression lives in systems too is understanding that systems don't change just because we identify them; they change because we disrupt them. This is a choice. Change is intentional. Allowing the system to run as it always has is also a choice—one that denies many students access to the opportunities that we have pledged our careers to creating.

Many of us look at these systems. We see their magnitude, and we question our ability to create any kind of real change. From where I teach, there are so many systems that I cannot influence yet. What impact can I make on residential and school segregation? How can I ensure equitable access to grade-level curriculum for my students with disabilities? How do I challenge antiquated grading systems, exclusive school discipline codes, or the unhealthy fixation on assessment? This has led me to ask, "What are the systems that I can influence right now?"

The answer: the ones that govern my classroom. For me, that disruption starts with these actions:

- ▣ Question the rules, policies, procedures, practices, and customs that define my classroom culture.
- ▣ Identify any groups in my classroom that consistently benefit less from the way things are.
- ▣ Change the way I do school so that the kids who belong to those groups have more opportunities to succeed.

Question the Things That Define Your Classroom Culture

To many of us, the culture of our schools or of our classrooms is invisible. It just *is*. It's how things are . . . how they have always been. Some of us know classroom culture to be how we greet each other or how we line up for recess or how we share snack—the rituals that we decide on in our grade teams or departments at the beginning of each term.

If we want to ensure that all kids benefit from the way that we choose to do school, we must realize that culture is not naturally occurring. We make it. Or it is thrust upon us. Either way, culture is visible and large and if we are not careful, our classroom and school culture can work to silence, exclude, and oppress children.

Classroom culture can be easier to see and work on if we ask a few illuminating questions first. Figure 2.1 shows a list of questions I ask myself when I want to examine the aspects of my classroom culture that are not always so easy to see.

Identify Any Groups That Consistently Benefit Less from the Way Things Are

When we look at school-related statistics—like the various achievement gaps—in STEAM-related subjects or in literacy or on national tests, we marvel puzzlingly at the reality that in some areas girls or people of color or poor kids or kids with disabilities or kids who speak more than one language sometimes net less of a positive result from academic programs.

" . . . I want to build a bridge for children— a bridge between what we are doing in class and the lives that they lead outside of class. I want to be able to show kids how each skill I teach in class makes life right now better outside of class."

Figure 2.1 *Classroom Culture Questions*

The Question
What specific things does a child have to do each day to be successful in this class? (I list them. I might even group them: habits, behaviors, academic skills, etc.) How is this communicated to children? How often? What structures exist to help them to do these things consistently?
In order to do those things, what do they have to know? Where are those things taught? How frequently do I give kids an opportunity to practice those understandings?
Of the things that children have to do to be successful, which among them mirror the kinds of things they already do as members of their unique communities or groups? Are these things named in class?
What are some ways I can make connections or parallels between in-class success criteria and the things that they already do to be successful in their lives outside of school?
Is there anything that might prevent any of my kids from regularly doing the things that lead to in-class success? How can I reimagine my success criteria so that all my children are included?
To help with reimagining what in-class success can look like, what are all the different ways that children can do each thing? Is there a particular way or method that a kid cannot use? Why is that particular method excluded?

What This Question Illuminates

This shows the specific criteria for success in my classroom. In many classrooms, kids aren't clear on what they have to do to be successful beyond "Do your work" and "Don't make the teacher mad." Thinking about this ahead of time gives children more control over their success.

These questions help me to make sure that I'm always giving kids consistent access to opportunities to be successful. In many classrooms, if a kid does not invest in our classroom culture early, by learning its structures in August or September, it's hard for them to catch up. Thinking through this helps me ensure there is always an opportunity for kids to invest in classroom culture.

I want to be able to name the powerful things that children know how to do *already*. Kids bring great insight with them to the classroom, and these questions allow me to consider that insight and to think about how I might show how that insight can have in-school benefits too. This kind of transference—what you know and do in life has school benefits too—is powerful and important.

Sometimes the things we value in the classroom are at odds with the things that children value outside of it. They do not have to be. Thinking about the work that kids are already doing in their families or in their neighborhoods helps me to make sure that the work I'm doing in my classroom supports the kind of lives kids want to lead outside of it.

If I construct a vision for success and a kid's economic status, race, gender, religion, or disability stands in the way of that success, then my classroom vision is exclusive and damaging to children. These questions position me to think and work in a way that is as inclusive as possible.

These questions help me to keep my mind open to possibility. Success is not limited to my vision of it. I want to be able to imagine classroom success expressing itself in lots of different ways and to create the space for kids to pursue it in a way that feels authentic to them.

When we talk about these results—outcomes of the various systems of teaching that we have devised—we often talk as if there is something wrong with the children.

Anytime an operating system—like a school or a curriculum—consistently fails a specific subset of people, there is not something wrong with the people (in this case, children). There is something wrong with the system—the institution or the curriculum.

To put it simply, if we were to devise a class, and all the kids with green eyes failed that class, we would not run around in circles blaming each other, vilifying the kids with green eyes and asking, "What is wrong with them or their parents?" Such a class would have been flawed, because there would have been something in it that prevented the success of a specific group of people. In such a case, the just thing to do would be to ask, "What is it about the way we do business in this class that creates conditions where many of the kids with green eyes fail?"

In this case, a powerful teacher would change the components of the class to give green-eyed kids a better chance at success.

We must do the same for girls, who are underrepresented in STEAM-related fields. We must do the same for black and Latino boys. We must do the same for poor children and for children with disabilities. Such a stance is essential if we are serious about reaching all of the groups that are marginalized by how we do school.

Inclusivity in the context of teaching and learning does not simply mean that "you are allowed to be present here." To be included means "we have changed ourselves and our practices to make 'here' a place where you can thrive." Justice in teaching does not live just at the school board or state level. Justice in teaching can be found in the very structures of our individual classrooms.

A kid can't be successful in my classroom if I have not created the opportunities for that child to be successful. Each decision that I make in the classroom is an opportunity created or denied. If I'm intentional about these choices, then my classroom can become a place where kids aren't just incidentally powerful but powerful by intentional design—in all the ways that we want them to grow.

When we consider school as it functions best, kids learn. When learning does not happen, it fails because there are things that get in the way. Lots of those things come from outside of the classroom, but a good number of them originate from within it. We can't take on the world's challenges without first acknowledging the structural boogeymen that live in our own classrooms. This work is not easy, but it is necessary.

We want students to succeed. When they don't, it bothers us.

That quest starts here.

1. Start by making a list of the kids that you worry about or those that you stay up late wondering about. Often, these are the students who work differently, whose behavior we find challenging, who don't complete classwork or homework, or whom we cannot seem to reach or engage.

2. Sort those children into groups, and give each group a name. You'll start to notice trends here, and your naming conventions will reflect those trends.

    a. You'll notice that you'll have groups like "the kids who speak two or more languages" or "the kids who are two grade levels below benchmark."

    b. Depending on where you work, you will notice that your groups may even have a specific ability, class, gender, or race dynamic. You might find that some of your outliers fall into groups like "the students who take the bus in the morning" or "my chatty boys."

    c. Do not ignore this. As we work to make schools better for all kids, we cannot ignore the reality that for many, school does not work because its mechanisms do not take into account the aspects of their identity that are not white, male, middle-class, or able-bodied.

3. What makes students successful in your class? Try to answer this question in no more than three sentences.

    a. Your answer might be something like: "One can be successful in this class by doing three things: . . ."

    b. Do all of your students know this? Do they understand it? How do you know?

4. For the kids that you listed in step 1, what barriers keep them from achieving the success that you just outlined? For many of us the barrier to success will be related to the kids' abilities. When

some people speak, they answer this question with a statement that starts something like "The kids in that group are not successful yet, because they can't . . ." As a rule, we don't want to make a habit of speaking about kids in terms of what they can't do. (We know that *can't* is a temporary condition defined by the things that we, the teachers, have not made opportunities for them to practice yet.) But if it helps you to organize your thinking now, you may start there.

Here is what that can look like in practice. Figure 2.2 shows a sheet that I bring to meetings. When we discuss children, I use it to make sure that the solutions that we imagine do not exclude kids because of their ability, race, class, gender, or approach to learning.

A blank template of the Thinking About the Kids in My Classroom sheet (Online Resource 2.1) can be found with the Companion Resources. Figure 2.3 shows what it looks like when I fill in the sheet.

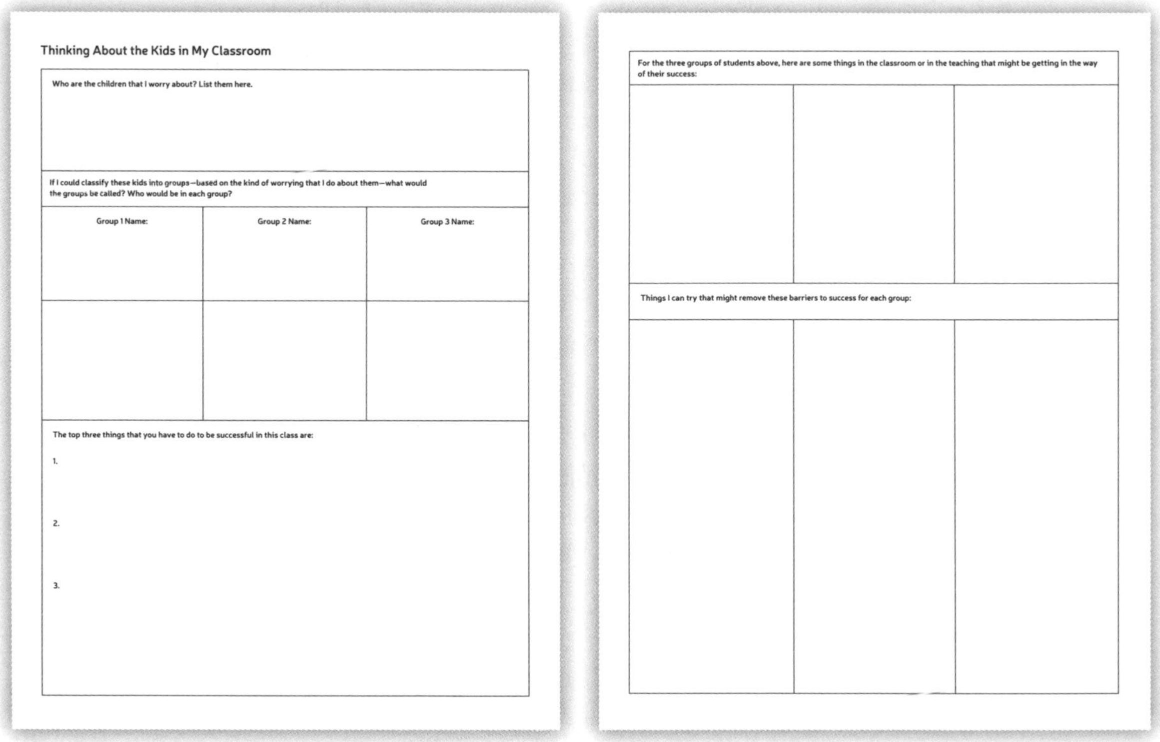

Figure 2.2 *Thinking About the Kids in My Classroom*

Figure 2.3 *Thinking About the Kids in My Classroom Sample*

Thinking About the Kids in My Classroom

Who are the children that I worry about? List them here.

First period: Scott, Travis, Elijah, Asia, Tykeem, Sandy, Jasmine, Keely

If I could classify these kids into groups—based on the kind of worrying that I do about them—what would the groups be called? Who would be in each group?

Group 1 Name:	Group 2 Name:	Group 3 Name:
The kids that are chronically late or absent	The kids that never seem to get it	The kids that TALK ALL THE TIME
Tykeem	Scott	Sandy
Keely	Travis	Jasmine
Elijah	Asia	Elijah
		Tykeem

The top three things that you have to do to be successful in this class are:

1. They have to participate in the lesson.

2. They have to do their classwork.

3. They have to read the books.

continues

Figure 2.3 *Thinking About the Kids in My Classroom Sample* (continued)

For the three groups of students above, here are some things in the classroom or in the teaching that might be getting in the way of their success:		
The late kids never get the lesson. That's three kids of twenty-five that miss the lesson at least three times a week. Basically, 12 percent of the kids miss 60 percent of the teaching or more.	The lessons right now are mostly lecture. They always seem overwhelmed. They don't seem to know what information is the most important to hold on to.	These kids need to move and socialize, and there just are not enough opportunities in the day to do so. So they create these opportunities for themselves.
Things I can try that might remove these barriers to success for each group:		
• In addition to working with them to get to school on time, I could give critical information or lessons later in the class period. • I can try to find out why getting to school is hard and give them tools to deal with or navigate those things.	• Maybe I can try to create lessons that have more modeling and more opportunities to try things firsthand. • I can implement more structured opportunities to work with peers. • I can work to eliminate the expectations that kids need to master a thing on the first try by creating lots of low-stakes opportunities to try things. • I can make visuals or charts that show the most important information, so that it's always on hand and kids don't have to memorize. I can teach them how to use these tools.	• I need to try building movement and talk breaks into the class. • I can try to channel a lot of the whole-class lecture into more intimate, targeted partner and small-group experiences. • I can find ways to utilize their voices in the classroom.

When we start to look at our classrooms this way, several things emerge. This approach is process-oriented. When I engage in this kind of thinking, I don't ever expect to walk away with a solution to the problems or challenges in my classroom. Instead, my goal after thinking or study is to have several ideas on hand to try. I also understand that these ideas won't work perfectly the first time. These are things that I will have to revisit and rethink. Our students don't need snake oil or miracle cures. They need careful, purposeful thinking. There is no one better suited to this work than us.

Change the Way You Do School So That Kids Have More Opportunities to Succeed

Once I have thought through the structural challenges that kids face in my classroom and I'm armed with ideas, the actual "now I've got to change my practice" part can be scary.

- Sometimes I don't know if I'm doing the right thing.

- I'm terrified of messing up. What if the kids don't get what they need because of me?

- What if I embarrass myself and I get called ableist or sexist or racist?

- What if I get in trouble at school for doing some unsanctioned new thing?

When it comes to this kind of justice work, transitioning beyond the thinking part to the doing part is where much of our work dies. Figure 2.4 is a chart that shows how each thing I want to try (from Figure 2.3) might change my practice.

When confronted with the unknown that is often associated with our deepest convictions and biggest dreams, it is much more comfortable to return to orthodoxy than it is to step into the void.

Figure 2.4 *Changing the Way I Do School*

Things I Can Try That Might Remove These Barriers to Success for Each Group
In addition to working with them to get to school on time, I could give critical information or lessons later in the class period.
I can try to find out why getting to school is hard and give them tools to deal with or navigate those things.
Maybe I can try to create lessons that have more modeling and more opportunities to try things firsthand.
I can implement more structured opportunities to work with peers.
I can work to eliminate the expectations that kids need to master a thing on the first try by creating lots of low-stakes opportunities to try things.
I can make visuals or charts that show the most important information, so that it's always on hand and kids don't have to memorize. I can teach them how to use these tools.
I need to try building movement and talk breaks into the class.
I can try to channel a lot of the whole-class lecture into more intimate, targeted partner and small-group experiences.
I can find ways to utilize their voices in the classroom.

How I Might Change My Practice So These Barriers Are Removed Permanently and the New Practices Become Part of Our Classroom Culture

I can rethink my practice in all my classes. I will consider teaching the lesson in the middle or end of class.

Right now, I will start to create tools that might help students get to school. I know I can use these tools every year. I will hand out a questionnaire asking students how they get to school each day. Once I collect and collate the information, I will hand out the tools to match the needs of each child. I want to remember to start my school year with this questionnaire.

Moving forward, all my lessons will feature active demonstration. After each demonstration, I can set kids up to try the thing immediately. It will also be important for me to remember that learning is iterative. I should never expect kids to get it on the first try. I can create space and time in my teaching for kids to have multiple tries at a thing.

Partnerships and groups come to mind immediately. I can structure my class to allow for kids to work with partners in some way each day. This means that I've got to spend some time cultivating and maintaining productive relationships. Also, I can act on the reality that not all relationships work. When a group is having a tough time, I can restructure that group without restructuring partnerships or groups across the whole class.

For each thing that I want kids to know, I can create several different kinds of opportunities for them to experience that thing firsthand. As of now, this means that just because I cover a thing does not mean that kids have mastery of the thing. I'm moving from the mind-set of "I covered it once" to the mind-set of "we practiced it several times."

Adding visuals to each lesson by using charts is an easy habit to start. Perhaps I can even recruit some student volunteers to help me make charts before school starts each morning. During lessons, I am committed to referencing the charts, so that kids can learn to use them independently.

I'm reconstructing my classroom rituals to include some kind of movement and talk at regular intervals. If those opportunities are always tied to the learning at hand, then kids won't lose any productivity.

Moving forward, I've got to talk less. Though it looks like kids are listening to me when I stand at the front of the room, they are not engaged with the learning. Making them an active part of classroom discourse means several things: less lecture from me and more trial and error and talk and experimentation from them.

Their voices do not belong just in their writing and schoolwork. They belong in my thinking and decision making. They belong in my grading policy and in my lesson planning and in the way that I showcase their accomplishments to real audiences beyond our classroom.

Status quo leaves too many of our children at the margins. I am not OK with suspension rates or dropout rates or literacy rates or employment levels. Save for an amazing and talented few, the people in power now look exactly like the people in power two hundred years ago. Education has done very little to shift power or to distribute it evenly. Rather, it has functioned to ensure that power stays where it has been—among the wealthy, among the men, among the white people. Our children and our communities do not need more business as usual. Our children need more of us to be comfortable with walking into the unknown.

When considering if I am doing the right thing, I've first got to define what the right thing is. To me, the right thing is any practice that gives children greater access to literacy, to math, to the arts, to science. To power.

In the context of a classroom, all I have to do is to think about the number of kids that had productive access to classwork or to conversations or to teaching and learning *before* I made a structural change. Then I think about the number of kids that have productive access after I have tried a new thing. If my new thing includes more children and engages them productively, then my new thing was the right thing.

You will make mistakes while on this path. I make them often, and I make them publicly. You will too. There will always be people who have lots to say about your thinking and your doing. I love inviting those people to the process. The only thing better than one practitioner working toward more inclusive practices is a whole community working toward greater inclusivity.

"Anytime an operating system—like a school or a curriculum—consistently fails a specific subset of people, there is not something wrong with the people (in this case, children). There is something wrong with the system—the institution or the curriculum."

3

Do Your Homework and Then Go for It

"I'm fighting to keep my head above water.
Now you're saying that I've also got to fight to
change the way my school does things!"

I HAD A PRINCIPAL THAT TERRIFIED ME. EVERY TIME HE ENTERED
my classroom or I encountered him in the hallway, I became—like many of the
students in his fiefdom—an eleven-year-old in a realm of adults. My thoughts
scrambled, my words stalled, and my eyes always sought a random spot on
the floor. In those days, I did not live to teach, I lived to survive—which meant
that I lived to please him.

I did not know him to be overtly mean-spirited or irrational, but he carried
his job title like a power tool. He was not interested in constructing teachers.
Rather, he fashioned perfect didactic cogs for his well-oiled machine. I was
untenured and inexperienced with a very small professional network. As such,
I could either be a cog or be homeless. Because of this reality, to me his vision of the world was biblical, and his hunches on how I should operate in it
were law.

When he spoke, there were only two paths; I could embrace fearful compliance or know crippling shame.

I searched for pockets of resistance. I found very few. Colleagues and I would talk about him at happy hour on Friday. Though this kept us sane, we would be right back to "Yes, sir!" at 7:50 on Monday morning. There is a brutal and awful majesty in watching a lion hunt an antelope. Similarly, it awed me to watch an entire building of adults submit to him—the same way that I did.

It broke me to watch an entire building of students do the same.

Unlike a lion, there was nothing natural about this. It did not have to be this way.

When we talked about children and their communities, it felt like an act of violence. We spoke of "those kids" and "their parents." We talked about "their values" not being the right ones, and we looked down upon their customs. Rarely was there talk of understanding or meeting people where they were or of co-constructing classroom and school culture. We loved talking about giving kids voice while mocking the voices that they brought to school with them.

Our favorite verbs to enact were obey, control, and punish. And we were good at it.

My baptism to this profession occurred in toxic waters. I tried to resist, but as an English teacher, I was attempting to teach kids to use their voices in a building that did not want to hear them. Though I did not know this at the time, the kids, astutely, did. Many of them had adopted a "Why bother?" attitude toward schooling. School, as we proffered it, did not know how to value kids that did not fit our narrowly constructed definition of normal.

The children knew the game. More importantly, they knew how to survive in it. Either be like "they" want you to be, or be silent, or be suspended. Those were the three options. When I would offer more inclusive or liberating alternatives, they would often decline, and true to my violent indoctrination, I never thought to understand why. I simply blamed them, saying, "They don't want to learn."

If you are not one of the "normal" ones, school is a dystopia.

Dystopian rule 1: Fail to fight an oppressive thing long enough, and you become it.

I, through compliance and silence, had become like my principal, a colonizer.

One critique of colonialism is that it assumes that the colonized are flawed. In a colonial paradigm, the colonized have nothing to offer the establishment. And the only way to save those who are flawed is to make them "normal," like "us." Colonizers are never overtly evil. With our books, our ways of doing things, and our money, we exist to "make things better." The cost of better? The erasure, denial, or suppression of what already exists, no matter how valuable those things are to the people that own them. This erasure is one kind of violence.

It is said that colonialism had (and still has) everything to teach and nothing to learn. The same critiques can be made of contemporary education—that we operate as if we have everything to teach kids and nothing to learn from them.

Fail to fight an oppressive thing long enough, and you become it. Here is one possible blueprint for that fight. Fortunately this is work that we do not necessarily have to do alone. Many of us are engaged in similar struggles.

Sometimes the things that we have to do become tradition, and as tradition ages sometimes those practices do not serve all children. Sometimes we have to change an established way of doing things in order to better serve our kids. Most times, changes that enrich the student experience are sought and welcomed, but sometimes the need for change surprises or eludes us altogether. What happens when you are one who notices that change needs to happen? What happens when others see your vision? What happens when they do not? What happens when your school is governed by the benevolent tenet "We've always done it this way"? What happens when your school is governed by more savage doctrines or individuals?

Proceed anyway.

Identify Why Change Needs to Happen

Sometimes a thing needs to change because it is not reaching students in the way I want to reach them. I may not be seeing the growth I want or the engagement that they need. When I notice such trends, I've got to ask myself some very important questions, like the ones in Figure 3.1. These questions can sometimes take weeks to answer, and that is OK. (After all, it takes time to become a hero.) Designing a powerful approach to a problem is potent change work.

Questions That Help Guide Change

What is it about this approach (method, lesson, expectation, mandate, etc.) that is not working *for students*? Be as specific as possible. Usually, when something is not working, you notice it first in two areas: student affect and student growth or performance.

| Affect: What are the students (not) doing that tells you this is not working? | Performance: How does student work reveal that this is not working? |

Is there anything about this approach that is not working for you or other teachers?

| Is this a matter of refinement—of teaching methods, of conditions of student work, or of resources (time, books, materials, etc.)? What do you need to manipulate or acquire? | Must the whole approach be changed? Why? Is the answer to the *why* in line with your values as an educator and your goals for kids? |

If the whole approach must be changed, ask yourself, "What are the ways that I need to overhaul it?"

| This could be more effective if I . . . | This could be more effective if I created conditions for the kids to . . . |

Figure 3.1 *Questions That Help Guide Change*

A blank template of the Questions That Help Guide Change chart (Online Resource 3.1) can be found with the Companion Resources.

Once I've asked myself these questions, I take a look around me. Am I in a place where it is safe for me to do change work openly? Do people here welcome new thinking? Is there a process or protocol for proposing new ideas to my group? Or could my venture be met with hostility? Whatever the answer, I know that I always need information to proceed.

Do a Little Bit of Research

Once you've decided that change needs to be made, it's important to think about the kind of change that would benefit your students most. This is where I usually have to be careful. It's easy to fall back on things that we know well or on the ways that we were taught when we were in school. It is important to ask, "Are those things really best for our students?"

Sometimes you'll have a hunch about what to do to make improvements. I like to follow that hunch into some light research by asking, "What are the people in my field thinking right now?" I use a template like the one in Figure 3.2.

This is not the time for "spend hours reading everything in the world" reading; this is you taking twenty minutes online to read up on your topic by browsing blogs, articles, and social media posts from *credible* people in the field. This is where reading a great professional book on your topic can help.

I've spent a lot of my career waiting for my supervisor, leader, or coach to tell me what to do or to give me the answers. My greatest professional heartbreaks typically occur when I discover that for whatever new challenge I'm facing, there is no certain single best answer or solution or approach other than to research quickly, try courageously, fail reflectively, stand up, and try again.

Sometimes I just want the answer. Maturing as a teacher has meant accepting that there is no such thing as just an answer. There is only inquiry. I have a question. I get as smart as I can about my issues. I choose a direction and I move. And I know that when I fail or when the solutions fail to serve me, I can simply choose a new direction and move again. Teaching is not absolute. It is always relative to how much I study and how courageously I make mistakes as I attempt to apply what I learn.

An Informal Research Template

	Answer 1	Answer 2	Answer 3
What are the professional organizations and groups that concern themselves with your subject?			
What are their websites and social media accounts?			
Use the search bar on the site to search for your topic. (It will yield books, articles, and posts.)			
Whom are they quoting or featuring on their social media?			
Search the internet or social media for the authors of those posts to find more materials.			
What do those people seem to be saying? (Understand that you won't always find resources—printables, lessons, etc. You don't want those anyway. They were not made for your students. You are looking for insight that will inform what *you* create.)			

Figure 3.2 *An Informal Research Template*

A blank template of the Informal Research chart (Online Resource 3.2) can be found with the Companion Resources.

Decide What to Do and Make a Plan

A little bit of research combined with your original hunch can be all you need to make a decision. If you are lucky enough to have a coach, mentor, or trusted colleague, you can talk to them about what you have learned so far. If you are in a situation where change is an articulated process, now is the time to get yourself on the agenda or ask for a meeting with the parties that can help you to realize your vision. If you are in a place where change might be met with various forms of hostility, this is when you use the research you just did to provision yourself for the journey ahead.

Once you've decided what you want to do, you've got to plan for it and prepare some of the materials you'll need to make it happen. When presenting your ideas to others, it helps to have a little bit of the work done in advance. This part is best done with a timer. Try not to let your planning and preparation exceed sixty minutes in this part, unless you are conducting a major curricular or programmatic overhaul.

When attempting individual or small-group change in this way, don't go large-scale yet. You don't yet have all the data that you'll need to support such a seismic shift. The first round of your planned change involves collecting the data that will lead to larger, more lasting changes later on. For now, there are a few things you need to do:

1. **Imagine how this change might happen.** Be real about the community where you work and think about how change usually happens. Whom will you need as an ally? What processes will you choose to follow or ignore? Is this process usually one where the community gathers around an idea, or do ideas usually float down from the top? Do people even care what happens in your classroom or will your ideas be opposed openly? Whatever your answers to these questions are, these first five steps in the change process happen alone or with a small team. Here, you'll be learning all about the change that you want to make. Does it even work? How does it impact kids? That way when you go to propose your change, you won't be proposing an idea. You'll be proposing data-informed practice.

2. **Select a small population of students to study.** You'll be attempting something that will potentially impact a whole class, but as you do, you'll want to have your eyes on certain students so that you can gauge and eventually communicate the impact that your work has on student growth. In a class of twenty-five to thirty-two students, I've historically chosen about five to study. You'll want to select students from across several groups so that you can test your work across the populations that constitute your classroom. I often think about selecting a student who is new to English, a student who might be performing below grade level, one who might be at or above grade level, and a kid who has an IEP that feels decently representative of the IEPs that I see most

often. Other groups might come to mind as you consider the changes that you want to make, but later on it will be imperative for you to communicate the impact that your work has had on the populations of students who need to grow the most.

3. **Make a five-day plan for how you will implement the changes you have chosen.** Five days feels like the right amount of time to give you a vision of what a large-scale version of this change can look like. During these five days, you can try everything, and you'll have enough time to begin to see some changes in your students, via their work, talk, affect, and thinking.

4. **Choose how you will measure the impact that your work is having on students.** Anyone can make change, but to make persisting change, we've got to be able to measure and articulate its value. It helps to collect student work and testimonials, from those in the groups that you have chosen to study. Additionally, having examples of the lesson plans that you used to guide students to this work is necessary for helping colleagues to embrace your innovation later on. You should be able to answer the questions, "Is this better for students than the other way?" and "If we do it this new way, can we make comparable gains?"

5. **Decide how you will share your findings.** Will it be in a department meeting? One-on-one with the department chair, team leader, or principal? Or will you float the idea to a representative so that they may take it to the school leaders for you? Are you preparing for some passionate debate, or a "do whatever you want" conversation, or a full-on fight?

Figure 3.3 offers a guide for how you can plan for change.

A blank template of the Guide for Planning Change Quickly (Online Resource 3.3) can be found with the Companion Resources.

Here's one possible way this might go: Let's say my school adopts a social studies textbook that comes with a curriculum that I'm not so sure about. The book comes with daily activities—copy the vocabulary words, listen to the lecture, take notes, read the chapter, answer the questions, define the words. Study the notes. Take the quiz. Rinse. Repeat.

Time	Task	Notes and Ideas
5 min	**Select the students whom you want to keep a close eye on during your trial. Some things to consider:** Which kids aren't growing as much under the current way of doing things? Which kids are not fully engaged in learning as it is? Which kids are those whose engagement you want to sustain? Which kids need you to think about ways of teaching that they can access?	
35 min	**Make your five-day plan. Some things to consider:** What will you teach *and show or model* each day? What will kids practice? How will you create multiple opportunities for that practice? How will kids give themselves feedback? How will you give kids feedback? How will kids practice again (and again) after feedback?	
10 min	**Create the assessments and tasks that you will collect as evidence. These should be as authentic as possible. Also consider your plan for interviewing students over the course of your planned week.**	
10 min	**Make your plan for how you will share your findings with the team.**	

A Guide for Planning Change Quickly

Figure 3.3 *A Guide for Planning Change Quickly*

The teacher's guide even suggests that I tell them what to think about the pictures and images in the book. This assumption that my students would not even know what to think when confronted with a picture as dramatically violent as one of the Boston Massacre really bothers me. I *feel* that I do not want to follow this way of teaching social studies, but this is what the team has decided on, and I play my position (and breaking rules scares me—as it does many of us), so . . . I invest all of my energy in following the teacher's guide.

My *feeling* that I would not like this curriculum becomes a belief before the second week of school is done. The kids are with me during language arts, but as soon as it is time for social studies, the complaints start. And if you know middle school, you also know that unaddressed complaints become talking out of turn, wandering around the room, "I just want to talk to my friend at the blue table," and "I just threw a paper ball at the blue table because even though we were best friends four minutes ago, I hate that guy now." Now I, the teacher, am fighting back tears. Not the sad or angry ones, but those tears that emerge only when stuff is 100 percent out of control.

This is not working for my students, and to be honest, any curriculum that features Cornelius crying on the floor as a daily closing activity does not work for me either. Two weeks into school, and I want to trash this curriculum and detonate this textbook. Forever. But I'm "just" a teacher. And my principal's power to radically influence my ability to pay my electric bill is scary as hell.

I do all the negative self-talk that we do when we are in impossible situations like this:

"What if it's not the curriculum? What if it's me? These kids need somebody stronger than me. I can't control my class."
"Eff that. It's not me. It's *them. I don't like these kids.* Because they are *all* conspiring against me. I see how they look at me when I pick them up from lunch. Their enmity for me is Shakespearean. I'd better beware the Ides of March . . . if I can survive until then."
"You know what?! It's not them. It's the *system.* This whole town expects them to fail. We don't get the funding or the support or the training or the resources that they get downtown. . . ."
"Actually, it's not the system; it's the parents . . . the clueless people on the school board . . . the administration . . . the neighborhood . . . the fact that I teach them after lunch . . ."

At times, all of those things can be devastatingly true. At times all of those things can be wildly untrue. None of those sentiments changes anything, though. The kids are still not engaged in the study of history. And I *can* change that. Figure 3.4 shows my possible thinking using the Questions That Help Guide Change (blank template found in Figure 3.1 and Online Resource 3.1).

One thing that seems to keep coming up here is that I want kids to participate more. Maybe I'll decide to change how the kids engage with the class by giving them more options for speaking, moving, sharing, and completing work. I need to do some fast research because I just don't know enough about managing student talk and other activities, and I don't want it to turn into a free-for-all. Figure 3.5 shows my possible thinking in the Informal Research Template (blank found in Figure 3.2 and Online Resource 3.2).

Now that I have all of these good ideas and suggestions, I've got to fashion them into a cohesive whole so that I'm not just supplementing a curriculum that does not work for my students with a bunch of random activities. Figure 3.6 shows my possible notes and ideas in the Planning Change Quickly guide (blank found in Figure 3.3 and Online Resource 3.3).

Execute the Plan

Try it. It won't all go well. That's to be expected, so you'll be making active revisions as you go. Observe everything, and reflect. Often.

When I'm in this part of my work, I try to remember that I'm doing this for my students, yes, but I'm potentially doing this for every student on the grade team or in the school, so I want to keep examples of everything and I want to start crafting the story of how this work came to be, why it came to be, and how it can go for everyone else.

> I've really been struggling with this textbook. When it was given to us, I studied it carefully. I recognize all the work and insight that went into writing and selecting it for the district. I taught my way through the first three chapters, and I was not seeing the level of engagement or student productivity that I wanted, so I asked myself, "I know my students well. How can I use that

Figure 3.4 *Questions That Help Guide Change Sample*

What is it about this approach [method, lesson, expectation, mandate, etc.] that is not working *for students*? Be as specific as possible. Usually, when something is not working, you notice it first in two areas: student affect and student growth or performance.

Affect: What are the kids (not) doing that tells you this is not working?	Performance: How does student work reveal that this is not working?
They are not interested at all. On good days, they are compliant, because they want to do well, but none of them cares about this material, so when they run out of energy for blind obedience, paper balls get thrown, kids are out of seats, no one listens, and arguments start.	Beyond the mindless copying that they do from the book, there is no real work. Everyone's notebook looks the same, because they all copy rote information from the same textbook. I can take the notebook from the most proficient kid in the class and it looks almost identical to the notebook from the kid who has only been speaking English for a year. There is no growth here. Only compliance.

Is there anything about this approach that is not working for you or other teachers?

This bores them, and then I've got to deal with all the discipline issues that arise as a result of that boredom. As it is now, they are learning very little history. Anything that I could do that would get more history into them OR reduce the amount office referrals would be a win.

Is this a matter refinement—of teaching methods, of conditions of student work, or of resources (time, books, materials, etc.)? What do you need to manipulate or acquire?	Must the whole approach be changed? Why? Is the answer to that *why* in line with your values as an educator and your goals for kids?
Maybe I can change some of the teaching methods in this curriculum. The textbook feels very assignment-driven; maybe I can create a few collaborative activities or have the kids read texts that are a bit more exciting.	This all feels like rote memorization to me. Maybe I can shift the focus a bit to more critical thinking. The kids really like questioning and challenging things and that is what REAL historians do anyway. Maybe I can include aspects of that in my remix of this textbook. Also, my kids are really into social issues. Maybe we can examine historical issues and figure out how we can use what we learn from them to solve contemporary issues. . . .

continues

Figure 3.4 *Questions That Help Guide Change Sample* (continued)

If the whole approach must be changed, ask yourself, "What are the ways that I need to overhaul it?"	
This could be more effective if I . . .	**This could be more effective if I created conditions for the kids to . . .**
▪ Taught specific reading and thinking skills that would help them to make the most sense of the content that they are encountering in their book.	▪ Talk, question, and debate each other.
▪ Tried to consider the most important parts of each unit . . . and cool ways to present it, so that they would not miss out on any of the content.	▪ Write real things that are not just summarizing or copying.
▪ Could figure out ways for the class to run in a more participatory way—hands-on activities, role-playing, etc. They are already out of their seats. Maybe I can come up with cool things for them to do while they are up.	▪ Read different kinds of text including maybe some cool multimedia stuff or even some primary sources.

knowledge and build on what the authors of this book have done?" Our kids are social. They learn a lot from each other. I decided to add more opportunities for kids to talk and more visual and experiential support.

I added a few opportunities to talk to each day's plan and I added opportunities for them to work with artifacts and visuals every day. I decided to test my additions for a week to see if they would help the kids to grasp the material better. Here are my findings. . . .

It helps others to see my vision if I can articulate my findings. I use an Articulation Plan like the one in Figure 3.7.

Figure 3.5 *Research Template Sample*

An Informal Research Sample

	Answer 1	Answer 2	Answer 3
What are the professional organizations and groups that concern themselves with your subject?	The Facing History and Ourselves organization does great work.	Zinn Education Project does a lot of work with history teachers. I flipped through one of their books once.	The Colonial Williamsburg organization hosts school groups to do hands-on activities. Maybe I can learn something.
What are their websites and social media accounts?	https://www.facinghistory.org https://twitter.com/facinghistory https://www.instagram.com/facinghistory/	https://www.zinnedproject.org/ https://twitter.com/ZinnEdProject	http://www.history.org/
Use the search bar on the site to search for your topic. (It will yield books, articles, and posts.)	This gives me lots of books and resources. I don't have time to buy all of these, but I noted several of the authors.	Lots of really cool ideas here. I downloaded some articles, which I'll read when I have more time.	There were lots of pictures here. Perhaps I can print those and use them for classroom activities later.
Whom are they quoting or featuring on their social media?			
Search the internet or social media for the authors of those posts to find more materials.	✓	✓	✓
What do those people seem to be saying? (Understand that you won't always find resources—printables, lessons, etc. You don't want those anyway. They were not made for your students. You are looking for insight that will inform what *you* create.)	They give me several ways I can look at history and think about issues that the kids are facing right now. This will be good for taking what the textbook presents and giving it a contemporary spin.	I've gotten so much insight about the people and perspectives that are not in our textbook. This can be great for maybe doing some point-of-view work with the kids. I know that they do that in language arts. This can be valuable in social studies too.	There is a lot here about encouraging kids to be real historians—to notice things, make guesses or theories, and support those theories with things that they discover from "reading" artifacts and primary texts like documents. We could do some really cool detective work with this.

Figure 3.6 *A Guide for Planning Change Quickly Sample*

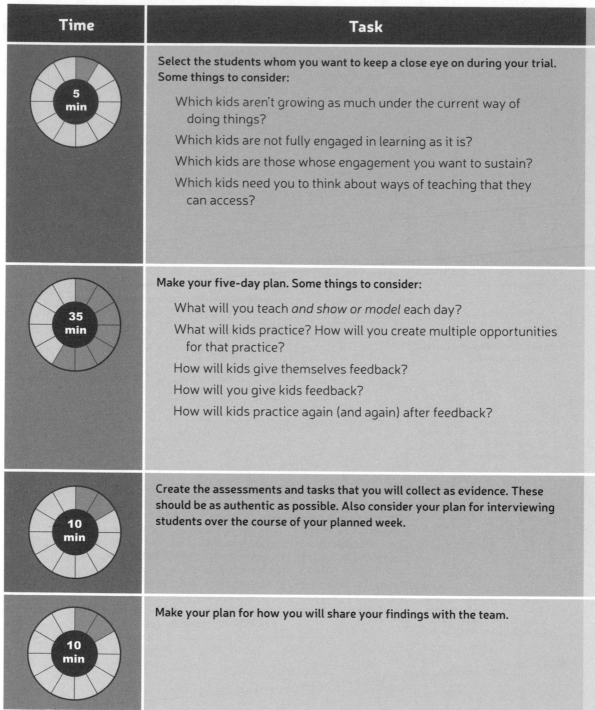

Time	Task
5 min	Select the students whom you want to keep a close eye on during your trial. Some things to consider:
	Which kids aren't growing as much under the current way of doing things?
	Which kids are not fully engaged in learning as it is?
	Which kids are those whose engagement you want to sustain?
	Which kids need you to think about ways of teaching that they can access?
35 min	Make your five-day plan. Some things to consider:
	What will you teach *and show or model* each day?
	What will kids practice? How will you create multiple opportunities for that practice?
	How will kids give themselves feedback?
	How will you give kids feedback?
	How will kids practice again (and again) after feedback?
10 min	Create the assessments and tasks that you will collect as evidence. These should be as authentic as possible. Also consider your plan for interviewing students over the course of your planned week.
10 min	Make your plan for how you will share your findings with the team.

Notes and Ideas

When I was fighting my way through the textbook, I could see Dan really trying to stay engaged, but the textbook experience was so powerfully mundane that he would check out habitually about fifteen minutes into class. I'll study Dan's response to my changes. He represents the population of kids that really want to learn but I just have not reached yet.

Samuel. According to him, he hates everything about school. Maybe he's right. I'm not sure yet, because I have not tried everything. I'll study Samuel's response to my changes. He does not resist learning, as he is a proficient learner in his neighborhood, in his Scout group, and on the basketball court. However, he has resisted my teaching. He represents my population of kids who resist teaching.

Rosa has an auditory processing disability. Listening for long periods of time does not work for her, so I need to present information in other ways to give her full access to each lesson. There are several kids like her in my grade. I want to study her response to my changes to make sure that my work is inclusive.

I want to make a plan that is not all about lecture, read textbook, answer questions, repeat. I'm thinking that I can start with a simple change. The kids love talking, so I'll start each day in a hands-on way by having kids study some artifact or media that connects to the lesson. They can generate ideas about the artifact and the time period based on what they experience. I'll use some specific talk protocols to keep the talk short and purposeful, and then we'll be able to use our shared insight to fuel the lesson.

This will reduce the time that I need to lecture, by replacing it with light inquiry. Additionally, this will allow them to enter the reading with background knowledge. I can supplement the reading with images and the opportunity to read in small groups.

Before we answer the questions at the end, I can create space for more discussion that will fuel the writing that they do in response to these questions.

In order to track the kids' progress with talk this week, I can record some of their conversations. Additionally, I can hold on to the answers that they produce in response to the questions that usually appear at the end of each section.

I can interview Dan, Samuel, and Rosa at the beginning of the week and at the end of the week to get their thoughts on how these small changes are working for them.

I can ask for three minutes at the end of our department meeting next week to share my findings, specifically the student work and the videos. I can compare these artifacts with some from previous weeks when kids were not as engaged. After sharing them, I can offer to support any of my colleagues who might need help adding talk and visual supports to our prescribed textbook curriculum.

An Articulation Plan for Saying What You Really Mean

Language You Can Use When Talking to Your Department, Team, School Leaders, and Mentors	Notes and Data You Will Need to Bring to a Conversation That Invites Change
"I was noticing this thing in my classroom. . . ."	What were you noticing in your classroom?
"And I started asking myself, 'What would happen if I changed it?'"	What changes were you considering?
"I was most worried about these groups of students. . . ."	Name the groups of students that you kept an eye on as you did this work.
"So I tried . . ."	Name what you did.
"Here is how the students responded."	List the top three things that students did in response to your work. Be sure to name any significant trends, especially those that are related to the groups of students about whom you were concerned.

Language You Can Use When Talking to Your Department, Team, School Leaders, and Mentors	Notes and Data You Will Need to Bring to a Conversation That Invites Change
"Here are some examples of what they did."	Show work that illustrates your findings.
"I would love to be able to get more students to _____. If you were teaching this, what would you add to what I've already got here?"	In this part you are admitting that your trial was not perfect. No trial ever is. You are also demonstrating a commitment to continuing your innovation, and you are inviting feedback. Even if others don't board your ship, you've indicated your plan to keep sailing, *and* you are moving forward by incorporating feedback from the major stakeholders. Important.
"I think that something like this would be useful for the grade team [department, school]. I would love to help organize an effort for us to pilot this together."	This is your pitch. Creating a change in your classroom impacts your students. Creating larger change can impact your whole school. I want the latter. If you're reading this, I think you want the same. This work will not be easy.

Figure 3.7 *An Articulation Plan for Saying What You Really Mean*

A blank template for An Articulation Plan for Saying What You Really Mean (Online Resource 3.4) can be found with the Companion Resources.

Figure 3.8 shows what it might have looked like when I reflected on my five-day experience and gathered all my data.

When people hear you talking like this, and they understand that you base your classroom decisions on research and on data generated from practice in your classroom, you'll find that they will listen to you more. This kind of leadership improves discourse across a whole teacher team. Others will notice your methods, and dialogue will become richer, because you'll raise the bar. When people try to float ideas without the research support and the experiential data, it just won't sound as convincing, because of the example that you set. Though conversations will be hard (conversations about authentic learning can't all be easy; meeting

Figure 3.8 *An Articulation Plan for Saying What You Really Mean Sample*

Language You Can Use When Talking to Your Department, Team, School Leaders, and Mentors	Notes and Data You Will Need to Bring to a Conversation That Invites Change
"I was noticing this thing in my classroom. . . ."	**What were you noticing in your classroom?** I was noticing that kids were not enthused by social studies at all. As such, they were learning very little. I could tell because their responses to questions on quizzes were static.
"And I started asking myself, 'What would happen if I changed it?'"	**What changes were you considering?** I wanted to create more opportunities for kids to talk instead of just being lectured at. Maybe I could introduce visuals and artifacts and primary sources too.
"I was most worried about these groups of students. . . ."	**Name the groups of students that you kept an eye on as you did this work.** I was particularly concerned because I was starting to lose the kids that normally choose to invest in everything. Of course, my students with disabilities are always on my mind, and I've got a few kids that profess to hate history, so I wanted to make sure that I was thinking about them too.

continues

Figure 3.8 *An Articulation Plan for Saying What You Really Mean Sample* (continued)

Language You Can Use When Talking to Your Department, Team, School Leaders, and Mentors	Notes and Data You Will Need to Bring to a Conversation That Invites Change

"So I tried . . ."

Name what you did.

I opened each class with a primary source or artifact that kids could study and talk about in groups. I kept the conversation brief, and I used it to frame the day's lecture and reading. I used a few academic databases and a Google image search to add picture support to my lectures, and I used some simple talk protocols to synthesize information before kids tried their writing task each day.

"Here is how the students responded."

List the top three things that students did in response to your work. Be sure to name any significant trends, especially those that are related to the groups of students about whom you were concerned.

The students all did more history. The gains were not earth-shattering, but they are doing more history than they were before, so that's a win for me! The group that made the biggest gains were my kids with IEPs. The discussion activities and picture support really helped. My students who hate history did not change their minds, but they participated more.

"Here are some examples of what they did."

Show work that illustrates your findings.

Here are responses to questions from students. You'll notice that the responses from last week are more robust. Here is some video of what the talk looked like; notice how invested the kids were in their partnerships. I've studied the video so that I can make the same moves again.

Language You Can Use When Talking to Your Department, Team, School Leaders, and Mentors	**Notes and Data You Will Need to Bring to a Conversation That Invites Change**

"I would love to be able to get more students to _____. If you were teaching this, what would you add to what I've already got here?"

In this part you are admitting that your trial was not perfect. No trial ever is. You are also demonstrating a commitment to continuing *your* innovation, and you are inviting feedback. Even if others don't board your ship, you've indicated your plan to keep sailing, *and* you are moving forward by incorporating feedback from the major stakeholders. Important.

I'm looking to create more opportunities for kids to talk. It really seemed to deepen their analysis. The more they talked, the better their writing. What would you suggest?

"I think that something like this would be useful for the grade team (department, school). I would love to help organize an effort for us to pilot this together."

This is your pitch. Creating a change in your classroom impacts your students. Creating larger change can impact your whole school. I want the latter. If you're reading this, I think you want the same. This work will not be easy.

I think that more talk in social studies is a simple way to get more intellectual work going in social studies, and it gives us a way to see that work. By pushing their talk forward, we are really pushing their thinking. All of the work that I've done in my classroom illuminates this trend. What's exciting is that this can happen schoolwide. Easily.

students where they are requires us to go places that we've never been), they will be productive. Change will take root, because you listened.

Find a Productive Way to Say No

After I learned to change things that were not going well, I started wondering if I had the kind of teacher bravery to say no to the things that I knew would not go well from the start. In most schools and for most leaders, that is a very different conversation.

How do I look at the person who, essentially, decides if I'll be able to pay my rent next month and say, "Thanks for that mandate, but naaw. I won't be doing it"?

Not like that.

No is such a powerful declaration. As teachers we don't use it enough.

The simplicity of the word *no* obscures the thoughtful complexity required to wield it. *No* is not just something that we can say in a meeting when an idea that we don't like surfaces. My *no* is rarely ever about the ideas that I dislike. As teachers, our *no* must be about potential paths or outcomes that do not meet the needs of our students. Because our students and their needs are dynamic, those paths shift and change. My *no* responses are similarly dynamic.

After a *no* response, people sometimes say, "Why the sudden *no*? You agreed to that thing last year! What has changed?"

The children I teach.

Every classroom decision is a statement of values. I value young people, their communities, their interests, and their goals. My *no* statements reflect this.

If I can tell from the onset that a thing is not going to be accessible to the children I teach, is not going to start with what they know, or is not going to value their identities or how they choose to engage with learning, with their peers, or with me, then my answer might still be yes. Because most of the things that come into my classroom can be altered, changed, or amended to work optimally for the children that I serve.

If that thing, for whatever reason, must be taught as is with no space for me and my team to mold it into what it needs to be for our kids, then that thing gets a one-week trial where we closely monitor student outcomes. If the outcomes are favorable, we swallow our initial misgivings and proceed. If the outcomes are not favorable, we use the process for change to pilot a week of changes, collect student data, and present our work as an alternative, using kid data to substantiate our choices. Our *no* responses must always come with alternatives.

Given what we know about fostering change, Figure 3.9 shows you how saying no can go.

Both of these approaches will yield alternatives to the advice or mandate that you were given. These alternatives will personify your *no*. It won't simply be an end to a conversation. Rather, your *no* will function as an exploration that deepens any discussion you are having about what to do next for children.

One time, the district suggested a reading intervention program to use with kids who were consistently not meeting grade-level standards. This is a group of kids that I think about all the time, so I was excited to learn more about the program.

At my next department meeting, the sales rep for the company revealed that this program would require us to move our most vulnerable readers into "grade-level complex texts" all of the time. He assured us that this "trial by fire" approach to reading would "toughen the kids up" and teach them to use grit in the face of adversity. "It's good for them," he assured.

I knew that it would not be.

This program did not consider my students' abilities. It did not have aspects they would find motivating. They would not understand the materials associated with this approach, and there was no room for choice— at all.

This was not a situation that I could turn away from. This was a programmatic investment that the school had already made. I understood this, so I had to think, "What kind of *no* is this? Is this a flexible *no* that will allow me to think about ways to make this intervention program more accessible to students while staying true to the overall integrity of the program? Or is this an inflexible *no*? Will I have to teach the program the best I can as is to see if the program itself proves my misgivings wrong or until I can collect enough reliable data to help my colleagues to see the shortcomings of the chosen approach?"

Guide to Saying No

When you receive a directive, a mandate, a request for action, a suggestion, or advice from colleagues, parents, stakeholders, or administrators, follow this thinking process:

First, assume that this thing comes from a great place. Though we may have different visions for success, we all want children to succeed.

Next, listen carefully to the advice. Try to hear the directive with your students in mind. Ask questions that will allow you to understand fully.

- Is this thing accessible to the children that I teach?
- Does it consider their abilities and preferences?
- Does it seem to motivate them or are there aspects of it that will help them to sustain interest when things get difficult?
- Are there enough supports to help them through the practices and tasks and allow them to meet the learning objectives?
- Can the students understand the materials associated with this approach?
- Does it value their personalities and backgrounds?
- Is there room for students to make some choices about how their learning unfolds?
- Does this meet the learning goals that I have co-constructed with and for my students?

Finally, choose a course of action based on your answers to these questions.

If you answered yes to most or all of these questions	If you answered no to most or all of these questions	If you're not allowed to customize this advice
Follow the advice!	Consider the advice. Think about what changes you'll need to make so that this piece of advice works optimally for your kids.

You can use the change protocol from earlier in this chapter to conduct a one-week pilot of your changes. Once you have incorporated all of your tweaks to the advice, follow it. | Follow it earnestly for a week using the change protocol from earlier in this chapter. Treat this advice as the change, and monitor how particular groups of students respond to it. Be careful here to not allow your skepticism to sabotage your work. Try earnestly. Collect student work, and pay close attention to see if the advice yields the kind of learning outcomes that you were hoping for. If it does, celebrate your new learning. If it does not, use the data that you collected to propose changes based on your good-faith first-week effort. |

Figure 3.9 *Guide to Saying No*

When I considered the situation fully, I realized that this was an inflexible *no*. I was not allowed to customize this mandate. So I committed to teaching it in good faith with a careful eye on student progress.

Less than ten days in, I had the data to prove my initial hunch correct. The whole department did. Students, parents, and teachers complained about the new approach. Beyond those complaints, I had ten days of detailed notes about the parts of the program that inspired aggressive reading growth and the parts that did not align with our students and our values. I was able to use this data to help the department to chart a more inclusive and accessible path forward.

You can use a similar approach to do the same. This work is not about saying no just because we do not like a thing. This is about carefully considering the needs of our students and using our *no* power to ensure that they get what they need.

"This work is not about saying no just because we do not like a thing. This is about carefully considering the needs of our students and using our no power to ensure that they get what they need."

PART 2

Taking Your
Dreams off
Deferment

There are several things that could cause one to leave a school board meeting in stunned, pensive silence.

We've all been to *that* meeting.

Fortunately for me, the meeting that I was leaving was not *that* kind of shocking. Rather, it was stunning in its beauty.

"Did you see those kids?" I marveled to my group of colleagues as we ambled out of the meeting and into the twilight.

The school board was moving resources in order to fund various equity programs all over town. A group of seventh graders attended the meeting and put themselves on the list of speakers. When it was their turn, each one of them used their time to talk to the board about a different way to use its institutional power to move beyond talk of equity and into the work of equity.

It was beautiful to watch each kid propose ideas for more gender inclusivity, for ending the persistent segregation in the district, and for expanding access to programs for disabled students and for students whose parents had lost their jobs.

"*Did you see those kids?!*" I repeated to my colleagues. Maybe they did not hear me the first time . . . it was going on 7:30 PM. Many of us had been on our feet since 8:00 AM and, like the sun, we were waning.

But I was energized by what I had just seen. Those students made claims, supported them with evidence, gave relevant examples, and used humor to convince a group of overtired adults that it wasn't enough to talk about access for all—it would have to be our business to make the programmatic shifts to actually ensure access for all.

Beautiful.

I want all kids to be able to communicate like that, I thought to myself.

Before I knew it, the words were tumbling, without filter, from my mouth. "*We* should do *that* with our students. We can teach essay writing through authentic advocacy! Those kids were no different than ours! Our kids have issues that matter, lives that matter. Our kids have stories to tell. *That could have been us!*"

They all looked at me and then at each other. Silence.

And then my department chair spoke first. "Cornelius, we can't teach like that because we've got to teach the curriculum. What would Mr. Bond say? Do you want him to come in for an observation and see you not teaching the cur-riculum and doing *that*?"

We have all heard this before.

I would love to share how I gathered myself and eloquently spoke about how teaching students to use written words to forge better lives for themselves *was* the curriculum. I would love to tell you how I explained that essay writing does not end with a test or a rubric but when kids can form principled argu-ments and engage in real advocacy for themselves and for others.

I did not do those things. It was 7:30 at the end of a long day. I missed my kids and my wife. So I swallowed that dream, turned toward the setting sun, and exhaled three exasperated words. "Yeah. You're right."

Dreams don't end when we wake from sleep. For many of us, some of our dreams end after meetings. At twilight.

Let's get free

In 1992, most of my fellow nerds were buying Marvel Comics' *X-Men* or Im-age's *Spawn*. I was into them too, but I spent most of my teenage money on Milestone Comics' *Hardware*. To this day, the opening panels of Hardware 1 are among the best things that I have ever read in English. I would argue that the titular character, Hardware, did not start out as a hero. He, like many, simply wanted freedom.

In the books, he built his reputation by taking the steps required to secure his personal freedom. That freedom eluded him until he learned to work toward the liberation of others. Month after month, I would read and learn with this pro-tagonist something that the writer, Dwayne McDuffie, spelled out in the opening pages of issue 1: many of us mistake being outside of cages for being free.

I came to teaching wanting to give kids tools to be free—free of the exter-nal structures and pitfalls that can rob young people of opportunity and free of the internal mind-sets and attitudes that can keep us mired to where we are instead of focused on where we can be.

Many of us came to teaching because we love kids and because we love science, history, art, books, or math. To love children is to love their futures. To desire disciplinary mastery is to desire mastery over mind-sets and attitudes. You and me; we are the same.

Others fight for freedom with legislation, with doctrine, or with military might. We do so with lessons and shared texts and questions and guided practice and love.

Yet, when I think back to that twilight conversation after the board meeting, I understand that I had somehow become a person willing to let dreams of freedom die because the curriculum did not allow it. This, too, is a thing that many of us have in common.

Some say that we have lost our aspirations to age, to practicality, and to wisdom.

I don't think we have lost our dreams. We have hidden them—caged them behind invisible bars—because we've got only twenty-four hours in a day, and we can't do it all, or because sometimes circumstances demand that we choose between doing what needs to be done (being a good teacher) and doing what we are told (being a good employee).

It does not have to be this way. We are not limited to these binary choices. We can still hope for and work toward powerful things, despite the working conditions at school or the challenges that clutter our path forward.

"Creating a space where kids feel safe means that we must create a space where we share power. One can let go of power without letting go of control."

4

Show Kids That You Hear Them

When it feels like the kids themselves are your nemesis:
"These principals and teacher-leaders don't know
my life! These kids can be so . . ."

LAST YEAR I WAS INVITED AS A SPEAKER TO MY FIRST EVER national teacher conference. Up until that point, most of my public speaking happened right after the morning announcements to the same group of thirteen-year-olds every day. Even at thirty-eight years old, this is the kind of thing you tell your family about. Mama gotta have something to brag to the church mothers about, right?

By the time I got around to showing my sister my face on the cover of the conference program, she trolled me in the way that only little sisters can. "People are going to pay hundreds of dollars to come see you?" she chortled lovingly. "Well you better fly out there and make us all proud, then," she continued, gesturing to my dad, who was beaming at the sight of our warm brand of sibling drama closing out its fourth decade. "I don't want nobody coming for me or Pop 'cause you made them want their money back."

The morning of my talk, echoes of that warning played on repeat across my nervous consciousness as I entered the hotel elevator. I was headed for my morning run. Exercise calms my nerves, and they needed calming. My sister's warning was drowning out the sound of Kendrick Lamar in my earbuds.

My mind summoned her voice again. "You better make us all proud." Nerves. This would need to be a long run. I zipped my hoodie with determined resolve.

Two floors into my descent, a woman entered the elevator. She did so in the anonymous way that strangers in expensive hotels occupy small elevators together. We made momentary eye contact and then averted our gaze to the glowing buttons counting down the floors. As we button-watched in silence, I noticed that she was holding the conference program. It was like a sign from the gods. People *were* willing to come see me. Here was one of them. I wasn't just relieved. I was excited.

I smiled broadly. "You're here for the literacy conference!" I exclaimed, and I pointed at her book. She clutched the book tightly to her chest and retreated to the opposite corner of the elevator. Her face contorted into a defensive grimace. "You don't know why I'm here . . . ," she began curtly.

Something was wrong. I did not know what.

And then, suddenly, I did. It took me less than a second to figure the social calculus of that moment.

"I'm a seventh-grade teacher," I reminded myself. My thoughts continued. Urgently. "I de-escalate problems all the time. I can fix this."

I leaned forward to show her my face on the cover of the book that she was holding, but I stopped mid-plea, understanding that this would be a no-win situation for me. I was wearing a hoodie and there was loud rap music tumbling from my headphones and I, a black man, was standing alone on an elevator with a scared white woman.

The elevator filled with the wordless tension between us. Before I could explain it away, my thoughts were interrupted by the sound of the doors opening. She brushed past me and fled into the lobby.

I let the doors close and button-watched back up to my room.

I gave my talk two hours later.

I am certain that I did not disappoint my sister. I could read it in the room. Several participants crowded me after the talk. Some wielded thoughtful questions or invitations to visit their schools. Others brought cameras for selfies or congratulatory handshakes. These were offerings I could not enjoy. First big talk of my career, and my mind was still on that elevator.

That woman was in this room. I wondered if she knew that I was in the room too. I wondered if she knew that the imposing person her mind had conjured and the easygoing teacher at the front of the auditorium were the same person. This was a great irony.

I contemplated her morning. After her hostile response to my greeting, she left me on the elevator, crossed the street to the convention center, and paid money to listen to me talk for an hour about student voice.

I wonder what she saw in that brief moment of eye contact on the elevator. I wonder what she saw when she regarded my face on the promotional materials for the conference. I wonder what she saw when she sat attentively somewhere in that ballroom-sized sea of teachers.

All of those wonderings are painfully rhetorical. I know what she saw in each instance. My mama and all the church mothers taught me how some people like her would see me—a pendulum swing from involuntary demonization to tolerance to fascination to earnest tokenizing.

For many, the theory of me is safe. I can be on a book or at a podium. I can be a concept. Multiculturalism. Voice. Inclusion. I can even be a representative. Black men. Africans. New Yorkers.

But for some of those same folks, the reality of me is threatening. I cannot be a person.

We can't share an elevator or a seat on the subway, and I certainly cannot surprise them by showing interest in a book.

My mind always goes to students—children. I wondered about *her* students of color. The theory of them was safe. In her classroom, how safe was their reality?

In the time it took me to utter one sentence, she read my clothing, my speech, and my body, and she inferred that I was an enemy. How long did it take her to read her students? If they didn't dress like they "should," speak like they "should," or show interest in the "right" things, did they become enemies too? As a profession, how quickly do we take kids and turn them into enemies?

What about our students with disabilities, our language learners, or our students who, for whatever reason, are different or defiant? We know that in some communities, six- and seven-year-olds feel that school is not for them. Where does that feeling come from?

Us. When we are tired, overworked, underprepared, or elsewhere altogether—which, for many of us, is every day. We know that kids are not the enemy. But it is not our knowing that betrays us. It's our implicit actions, our snap judgments, and our involuntary responses. How can we keep from acting like that?

We've got to *listen* to them.

Especially when it's clear that they are not listening to us.

Sometimes I wish they would stop texting, talking, walking around the room, calling out, throwing things . . . and just listen to *me*.

When I peer beneath the surface of their behavior, several things come into view. One thing is clear. *The kids are not my enemy.* Even when it feels like they are gleefully sabotaging my attempts at teaching (fifth period, every day, every seventh-grade classroom in America), they are, in myriad ways, simply responding to the things in their world in the best ways they know how. All of the children in our schools, especially the behavioral outliers, are simply trying to cope with all the input that home, school, hormones, and the world are handing them.

> *"We've got to listen to them. Especially when it's clear that they are not listening to us."*

When I plan lessons, one of the questions that I sometimes ask myself is, "What can I say or do that will get the kids to listen to me?" I'm trying to outgrow myself in this area. Though sometimes that question can lead me to lessons that kids endure, it does not lead me to lessons that kids love.

Though it can start there, "listening to me" is not the extent of the learning that kids can do in a classroom. Learning is something that kids have to elect to do, and I can make it easier for them to choose me and my teaching if my teaching is rooted in a few broad understandings:

Sometimes kids feel like what we are teaching is not for them.

Learning is inherently social, and sometimes the way that we run our classrooms is not.

Part of learning is making mistakes and testing authority, and sometimes we do not allow for that. At all. So kids find ways to do it anyway.

Even if we do not mean to, sometimes we are (or we represent) an authority that seeks to oppress, silence, or erase kids, their families, and their communities. Kids fight that oppression. Openly. By fighting us.

Sometimes kids don't feel like the classroom is safe for learning. Some kids don't feel like learning is a safe pursuit, period.

So how do I actually listen to a kid? So much work goes into listening. It does not start at the site of the conversation. It starts when you work toward creating the context for rich dialogue to happen. You need to create and maintain the kind of community that will help kids feel safe enough to be honest with you.

In a classroom, the teacher has a lot of power. That power is expressed and asserts itself in several ways. We get most of the attention. We make the rules, and in the ways that count most immediately to students, we decide the fate of each being and endeavor in the space. Though they can't always articulate it, when kids interrupt, disrupt, or stop our proceedings altogether, what they are really doing is attempting to take some of that power.

Though it might feel like they are, children are not primarily doing this to further some nefarious plot or agenda. Many children choose to disrupt because they legitimately have something to express, and traditional classroom power dynamics do not typically allow them the space to be heard in ways that they can readily recognize. So they find a way to make that space.

Creating a space where kids feel safe means that we must create a space where we share power. One can let go of power without letting go of control. Here are some ways to get this done:

Designate specific kids who can give you feedback. Help them to understand why you chose them. Be public with this information.

Plan for and hold regular class meetings to maintain community.

Shift from a punitive to an instructive mind-set.

Plan for and Hold Regular Class Meetings to Maintain Community

A class meeting does not have to be a big production. As our schedules get packed with more and more stuff, they shouldn't be. Instead, we can work them into other structures, transitions, or even content. These class meetings exist for the explicit purpose of maintaining community. Kids want to be powerful, and these meetings function as a site where that power can live and grow in a democratic way.

There are other kinds of class meetings that people hold to introduce concepts, address an issue, start an initiative, or work toward consensus. This is not one of those types of meetings. This class meeting is the classroom equivalent of an oil change: routine maintenance. In each class meeting, I try to accomplish two things:

> I want to introduce an idea.

> I want to listen to their thoughts about the idea.

This class meeting might happen in line as we walk to lunch or the gym; it might happen on the bus on the way to a field trip or during a class transition from one activity to the next. If I have done this well, the kids don't even know that we've had a "meeting." This should feel like we're just talking. Because we are. Relationship building must be intentional.

I try to vary the nature of these class meetings. I start the year with low-stakes topics, and I address weightier topics as the kids get used to sharing ideas together. These meetings typically last no longer than seven minutes and I try to have at least three a week at regular times.

I usually plan these meetings in a series, leaving gaps for cool topics that might come up. Additionally, I think about my meeting follow-up. What will I do with what I learn from children? See Figure 4.1 for an example of how a series of meetings might go. You'll see here how I use casual talk to engage the kids in school and community issues. I also use these meetings to deliberately build our capacity to talk about weightier topics as a community.

Though it is not public (these meetings feel off the cuff to students), the agenda for these meetings flows fast to keep them brief and dynamic. Figure 4.2 shows a quick structure for how these meetings can go.

These meetings do more than feed you information. They give your students the experience of being heard. Being heard affirms one's dignity and makes the classroom a safer place to learn. Also, these meetings are a way to bring social, community, or classroom issues to your community in a small way before introducing them in a larger way later on. This allows students to see you turning what you learn from them into longer, more meaningful classroom conversations and sustainable classroom practice.

Example of How a Series of Class Meetings Might Go

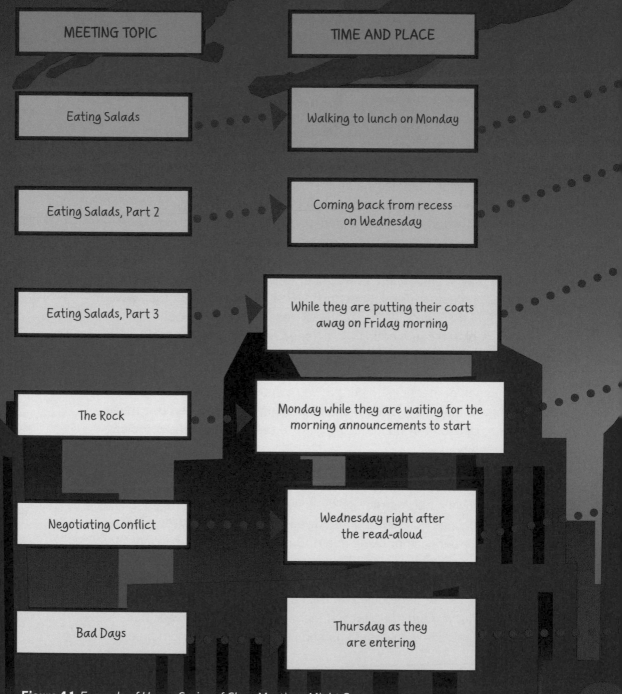

MEETING TOPIC	TIME AND PLACE
Eating Salads	Walking to lunch on Monday
Eating Salads, Part 2	Coming back from recess on Wednesday
Eating Salads, Part 3	While they are putting their coats away on Friday morning
The Rock	Monday while they are waiting for the morning announcements to start
Negotiating Conflict	Wednesday right after the read-aloud
Bad Days	Thursday as they are entering

Figure 4.1 *Example of How a Series of Class Meetings Might Go*

WHAT WILL I SAY TO INTRODUCE THE TOPIC? (USUALLY A QUESTION)	PLAN TO FOLLOW UP WITH WHAT I LEARN IN THE MEETING: WHAT WILL I *DO* WITH THIS INFO?

"Did anybody try the new salads last week? Were they good? What toppings do you put on salads?"

"I saw a show that said that eating salads makes you faster and stronger. I want to test that to see if it's true. Do you think that's something we can try during recess? How could we do that?"

I want to figure out how to get them to eat less junk food by figuring out a way to make salads attractive. Also, I want to make wellness a thing that they get used to talking about. This informal conversation is a good start.

I want to hear what they think about the idea, and I want to see if they can design an experiment.

"Today a few of you said that you were going to start the salad challenge. We'll run today and measure our time. We'll eat salads and then run again next week to see if we are faster. Who wants to try it? Should I try it too?"

Some kids will volunteer; some kids will not. That part does not matter much to me now. Really, I want them collaborating on a low-stakes project together. This is not an assignment. I just want to watch them work and plan organically. I can use what I learn here later in the year when planning other projects.

"All week last week, you all were talking to me about the Rock. I really want to watch one of his movies. Which one should I see? Why? What other actors should I be checking for?"

I want to listen to reasons why they like movies. This can help me to understand why they like books.

"In this book the characters had trouble. I'm having trouble understanding my sister. We're trying to decide what to do for the weekend. I want to go to a movie and she wants to go bowling. Every time we talk about it, we end up fighting. I don't want to fight anymore, but I really don't want to go bowling, and I'm going to see her after school. What should I do?"

I want to hear how they think through resolving conflicts. I can write some of their ideas down and perhaps use them later on when we encounter in-class conflicts that we need to work through.

"You know how some mornings, you wake up, and you kinda know it's going to be a tough day? I think I had one of those mornings, and I don't want it to be a tough day. I want to change how the day is going. One idea that I had to change my day was to start the day by drinking my favorite juice. Do you all have any other ideas?"

Kids get in a funk sometimes, and I want to model how to work oneself out of one, and I want to listen for ideas and strategies that they might have to do the same. Emotional regulation is tough work for kids, and this can give us a chance to make that work visible.

Figure 4.2 *A Possible Structure for Class Meetings*

Meeting Component	Length of Time	What I Might Say or Do
Opening question	< 1 minute	"Hi, you all, I was wondering . . . ," or "What do you all think about . . . ?" or "What would happen if . . . ?"
Instructions and discussion: Give the children clear instructions for how the discussion will go. Allow them to discuss quickly.	< 1 minute	"Discuss that for forty-five seconds with the person closest to you in line," or "Check in with the three other people at your table. The person closest to the door should talk first."
Listening and note-taking	2 minutes	Make sure that the kids see you leaning in and taking notes.
Recap to close	30 seconds	"So what you all are telling me is . . ." Make sure that the kids see you writing things down.
Reflection Think about how you will use what you learn from kids. Ask yourself: How will I use what I learn here to influence my teaching and my being tomorrow?		

When children see and understand that their voices can change a classroom, they begin to internalize the reality that their voices can change a community, a country, and a world.

Designate Specific Kids Who Can Give You Feedback

When we run into trouble, we rightfully seek help and feedback from other teachers. We can expand our support networks to include children. Teaching is for them, and when we need help with it, what kids think is essential.

We often say that kids' voices and ideas are important. This gives us an opportunity to show them. I like to tell children specifically why their ideas matter. This and how the practice of giving feedback to a teacher can help them later in life. I say things like:

- I've seen you start really important conversations in the cafeteria, and I would love your help having some important conversations in our classroom.

- One thing that kids your age want to get good at is being able to talk to adults about what they want or need in life. You are totally ready for that. We can practice that together in this classroom.

- You have so many ideas about things that we can do to make this classroom better for kids. You are the perfect person to help me as I try to do more for kids.

I often extend the invitation for children to give me feedback in public, making sure they understand why I chose them. I allow them to actually deliver the feedback privately or semiprivately in a one-on-one or small-group conversation at their desks.

Coaches, administrators, and other school leaders spend years learning how to give feedback that changes practice. Children do not have the luxury of this study. Their feedback will often be unrefined, but that does not make it any less valuable.

This act of soliciting feedback serves two very specific social purposes in your classroom.

Children see you trying to get better at something. They begin to understand the labor and intentionality required to improve. To kids, improvement can seem magical. Like something accidental over which we have no control. Watching you receive and incorporate feedback from their peers gives students a realistic blueprint for building a personal vision and realizing that vision through consistent work.

When you deputize students to give you critical feedback it means that you value them. Even when one student gives you feedback, and you listen, you are sending the message to all the children who witness that interaction that kids matter here.

I typically ask kids to give me feedback in three areas at first—use of time, the clarity of my demonstrations, and how well my assignments and assessments are constructed—but as I get to know them better, they are able to comment on so much more. Figure 4.3 shows how I ask for feedback on my use of time.

Inviting feedback on your use of time is a ritual that you can enact every day for a week before you graduate kids to giving other types of feedback. Each day, choose a different person to support you, and be sure to thank the kids publicly for their services. As the kids work throughout the week, also be sure to chat with your timekeepers privately or in small groups for advice on how you can make your lessons go faster so that you don't always run out of time. This will keep your lessons lean and your kids invested, and it will begin to build trust that you can warehouse for

Figure 4.3 *How I Ask for Student Feedback on My Use of Time*

WHAT I SAY TO INVITE FEEDBACK

"I'm really trying to be the kind of teacher who does not waste your time in class. Each day I'm going to try to teach my lesson in a very specific amount of time. Trevor, today I want to teach my lesson in ten minutes, because you all will be working independently for thirty minutes of our class time. Here's a stopwatch. Can you tell me when I have one minute left?

"The rest of you, I really need you with me during this lesson, because Trevor is going to be on me to keep things moving."

HOW I HONOR THE FEEDBACK

This invitation to feedback gives kids a road map for how the class will unfold. (You can even put it on a chart.) Sometimes kids choose to disrupt learning when class takes a surprising turn. If their teacher wants them to do something that they did not anticipate, in many scenarios it is safer to disrupt class than to take a social risk. When you give kids a road map, there are no surprises.

When Trevor alerts me, it is important here to stop my lesson when I promised that I would. As teachers we often undermine our own credibility when we use clichés like "five minutes." If we say something is going to last five minutes, it should last five minutes. Kids learn to undermine us sometimes because we undermine ourselves.

bigger issues and undertakings later on. In all honesty, I don't really need a timekeeper, but when building classroom community, the public sharing of power matters.

Figure 4.4 shows how I ask for feedback on the clarity of my demonstrations.

Again, this is a ritual that you can enact every day for some time before you graduate kids to giving other types of feedback. Each day, choose a different person to support you, and be sure to thank the kids publicly for their work. Then you can engage your supporters privately or in small groups for advice on how you can make your lessons more demonstrative.

Figure 4.4 *How I Ask for Student Feedback on the Clarity of My Demonstrations*

WHAT I SAY TO INVITE FEEDBACK

"There are lots of people who are teaching experts, and one of the things that they say is that you can learn more if I show you how to do a thing instead of just telling you, so in today's lesson, I'm really going to try to show you things and not just tell you.

"Raven, I'm excited about these new teaching moves. Can you watch me to make sure that whenever I explain something, I also *show* how to do it? Whenever you see me just talking, and not showing, could you raise your hand and remind me that the lesson would go better if I showed you how to do it?

"Everyone else, watch this. Today I want to show you that . . ."

HOW I HONOR THE FEEDBACK

This invitation to feedback alerts kids that they will get to see a thing in addition to just hearing about it. It turns their attention to the parts of your teaching that are demonstrative.

When Raven alerts me, it is important to stop talking, pause to think about what I want kids to actually do, and then to show it. A good start is, "I want you to . . . So watch me while I . . . Did you notice how I . . . ?"

A lot of teaching has been reduced to telling, and this frustrates students. They can withdraw from learning when we go into telling mode. Safeguarding against this keeps your teaching accessible for learners.

Finally, Figure 4.5 shows how I ask for feedback on how well my assignments and assessments are constructed.

Feedback on assignments and assessments is a ritual you can enact daily, and then each subsequent day, you can announce the small changes that you are making as the result of their feedback from the day before. As you make these announcements, be sure to give credit to the kids that gave you that specific feedback.

"Class, yesterday Daniel suggested that writing with dry-erase markers on the tabletops would be an excellent way for us to actually see the math. So we are trying it that way today. Thanks, Daniel."

Figure 4.5 *How I Ask for Student Feedback on How Well My Assignments and Assessments Are Constructed*

WHAT I SAY TO INVITE FEEDBACK

"I've been thinking lots about the kinds of assignments that I give. I've been studying with a lot of other teachers, and one of the things that we are learning is that school-work is supposed to be something that gives you enough practice at the things that we are learning so that you can get good at them.

"While you are doing the work today, I'm going to make time for you to talk with the people at your table. There are three things I want you to discuss during that time. I'm putting them on the board."

1. How is this assignment helping you to get good at doing this thing independently?

2. How could I change the assignment to make this a better practice experience?

3. Do you know of any materials that you could use that would help you to do this work better?

HOW I HONOR THE FEEDBACK

This invitation to feedback gives kids a voice in determining how their work can unfold. Sometimes kids choose to disrupt learning when the practice experiences are not accessible or when they do not speak to them. If their teacher wants them to do something that does not inspire or move them, the sensible thing to do is to think about something that does (this is what any smart adult would do); for kids, that thing is often not school-related. We know how this unfolds. We blame them for being off-task, and a simple engagement issue has the potential to become a discipline issue, and when it comes to discipline issues, kids lose (disproportionately so if they are children of color). We can prevent these losses by actually listening to kids.

When the kids start their work, give them a little bit of time to ease into their tasks. After about seven minutes of earnest work, you will feel the energy of the classroom shift. Kids will be a little less productive and more chatty. Use that shift as an opportunity for them to start their first reflections.

This makes the work of cocreating classroom culture visible to kids. We are not just saying that kid voices matter; we are showing them how they do. We are listening to them and making visible changes in response to what we're hearing.

After these three initial types of feedback, children will be conditioned to talking about your teaching and asking you to change it to suit their learning needs. One of the greatest gifts that we can give children is the ability to advocate for themselves and for their own education. Sending a child into the next grade or to middle school or high school or even college armed with the confidence to ask a teacher to change an aspect of teaching that could potentially amplify the learning for all students is an act of incredible beauty and ultimate empowerment.

Shift from a Punitive to an Instructive Mind-Set

There are kids sitting in classrooms who when asked, "What does it take to be successful in this classroom?" cannot answer the question beyond, "Be quiet? Sit still, maybe? Do what I'm told?" This is not their shortcoming. It is ours. We often assume that kids know and have what it takes to succeed in our classes. This is a dangerous assumption to make, because it leaves so many children without a way to access success.

There has been so much written about classroom management. When people come to observe my teaching, it is the thing that people ask me about the most. Coincidentally, save for a few extreme cases each year, classroom management is the thing that I think about the least.

When I think about kids, I have a belief that I don't share often enough. I am not interested in raising a nation of well-behaved children. At all. So that is not something I seek in my teaching. I want them to assert their presence. I want them to challenge my ideas. I want them to believe in and act upon their greatness, and I want them to understand that, while school does value these things, they are not great because of their grades or their accomplishments.

I want kids to understand that they are great and worthy of attention and time and love simply because they are human. In my classes, these are not things that I want kids to feel like they have to earn by being "good."

If how to be quiet and still is all kids have learned from us, then we have failed them in the worst way. There is not a single challenge in life that can be overcome by this kind of passive inaction. Being quiet and sitting still are not the blueprint for success in any context. They are a direct pathway to being overlooked and taken advantage of. To commit to "Be quiet. Sit still" as a classroom strategy is to educate children into insignificance.

Similarly, there are children who do not know the things that undermine a group's or an individual's immediate success. We can be better at teaching this.

Each week I remind kids of two things:

We will be successful this week if you . . .

The things that can slow our progress this week are . . . [These are my top three triggers.]

I try to keep each list limited to three items, and from week to week depending on the needs of the class community, I might change an item or two.

This is the work of moving away from a punitive mind-set toward a more instructive mind-set. I've got to rehearse and practice myself away from "remind and punish" and toward "correct and teach"—the state of classroom being where I understand that kids will be challenging (sometimes excessively so) and I've already rehearsed my affective response and the instructive moves that will usher kids back toward the thinking, talking, writing, and reading that I want them to do.

It is said that no firefighter is ever surprised that there is a fire. They expect them. The nature of fires, their severity, and their causes are all unique, but despite this, firefighters have an affective and tactical response to them. In the moment, they assess and prioritize threats. Not every flame is a five-alarm fire. These assessments and responses are rehearsed. What few people see is that much of a firefighter's work is in prevention and reflection—safety education, inspection, building codes, and emergency prep.

So it can be with us. Not every student disruption warrants a five-alarm response. We can evaluate disruptions and respond consistently. The thinking that says, "Make a huge deal out of the little things like walking in line, so that they will never get to the big things like hitting," is understandable but radically flawed. It assumes that kids default to this kind of negative or offensive behavior. They don't. Additionally, it establishes a dynamic that is more conducive to compliance than to community and it forces us into the taxing and oppressive position of being a warden rather than a pedagogue. Far too many of us are valued for our ability to control the kids, not for our ability to grow powerful mathematicians, scientists, historians, or communicators.

Figure 4.6 is a tool that I use to plan my journey out of a punitive mind-set, even in the most disruptive classrooms. I start by naming my expectations and my triggers to myself. I also choose how I will respond to these things, ahead of time. If the first time I think about or rehearse my response is at the site of the infraction, then I've already lost.

A blank template of Blueprint for Shifting Your Mind-Set from Punitive to Proactive (Online Resource 4.1) can be found with the Companion Resources.

Figure 4.7 is an example of how I've used the blueprint proactively.

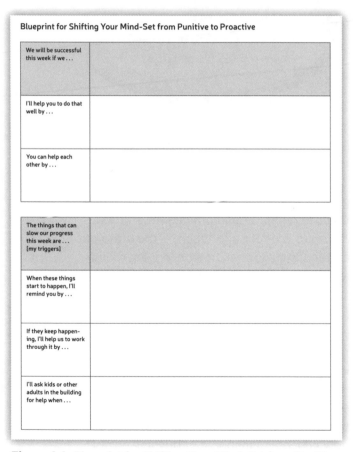

Figure 4.6 *Blueprint for Shifting Your Mind-Set from Punitive to Proactive*

After choosing what I want to do in each of these cases, I've got to rehearse two things:

- ▣ letting go of the things that are not on my top three (What will that look like? How will I signal to kids that these are unacceptable behaviors too without breaking my teaching stride?)

- ▣ responding to the things on my top three in ways that do not humiliate students

My rehearsal includes parts that I try at home, but I also run through dress rehearsals with the kids. When I work on my response at home, I'm attentive to my language. I want to make sure that my language does the following:

centers how children feel, especially if they have been the victim of any offending behavior

considers a kid's needs, abilities, and social functioning

discusses the behavior and not the child

is firm and fair

offers alternatives and next steps, not just consequences

moves us back toward learning

de-escalates rather than escalates

reflects my knowledge that a teacher's response to a classroom situation can be as disruptive to learning as the situation itself; I don't ever want to make a scene

Blueprint for Shifting Your Mind-Set from Punitive to Proactive Sample

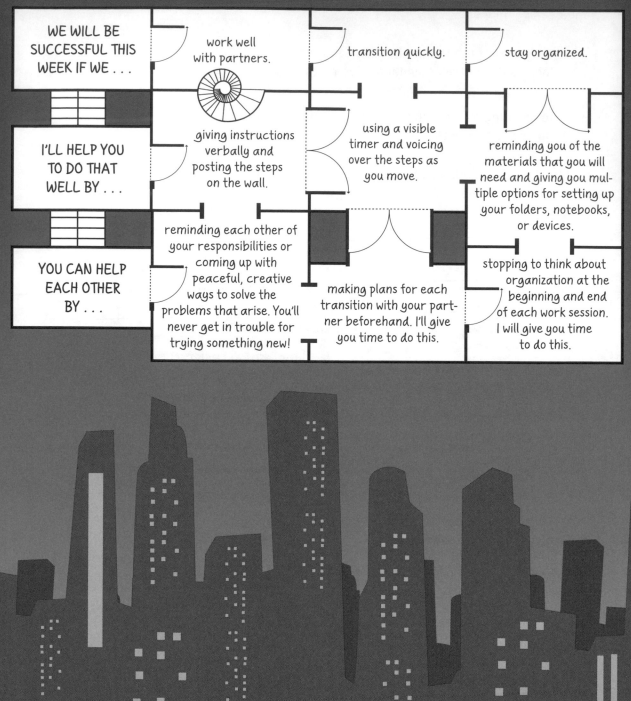

WE WILL BE SUCCESSFUL THIS WEEK IF WE . . .

work well with partners.

transition quickly.

stay organized.

I'LL HELP YOU TO DO THAT WELL BY . . .

giving instructions verbally and posting the steps on the wall.

using a visible timer and voicing over the steps as you move.

reminding you of the materials that you will need and giving you multiple options for setting up your folders, notebooks, or devices.

YOU CAN HELP EACH OTHER BY . . .

reminding each other of your responsibilities or coming up with peaceful, creative ways to solve the problems that arise. You'll never get in trouble for trying something new!

making plans for each transition with your partner beforehand. I'll give you time to do this.

stopping to think about organization at the beginning and end of each work session. I will give you time to do this.

Figure 4.7 *Blueprint for Shifting Your Mind-Set from Punitive to Proactive Sample*

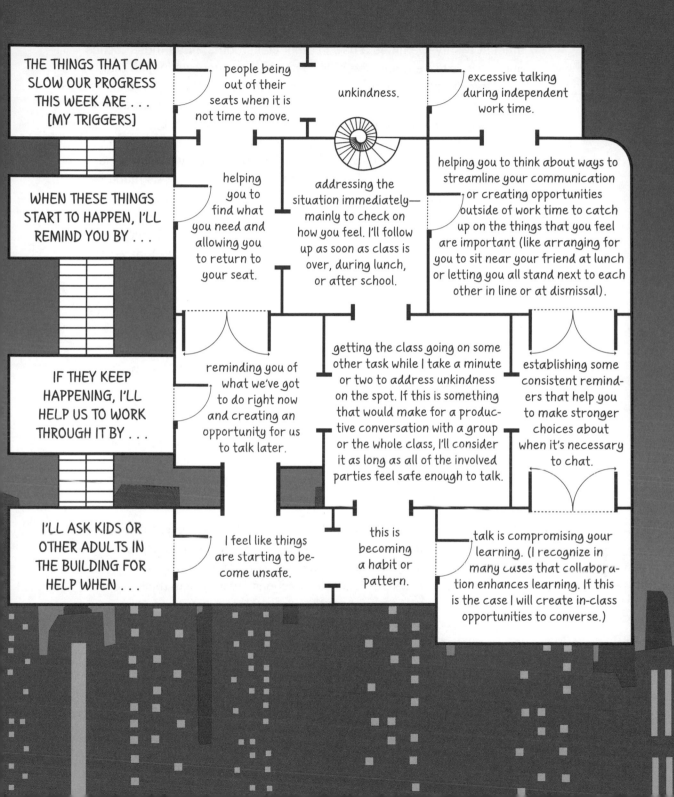

In some classrooms these are things that I end up saying and doing at least twenty-five times a day. In other classrooms, I use these tactics only once or twice a semester. No matter the frequency, I'm glad that I think through student behaviors and my response to them ahead of time. The peace of mind that this practice affords me frees up the emotional and intellectual energy that should be dedicated to teaching.

It is OK to have a couple of go-to catchphrases or sayings. We all remember things that our own teachers said over and over again. The powerful thing about those sayings is this: though some of us made fun of them, for the most part, we observed them—and we remember them. Figure 4.8 shows a few I have found particularly useful. Hopefully this will give you some ideas for the kinds of responses that you can have to disruptions that fall outside of your top three. The message that we must get across? "This behavior takes away from our learning and threatens the safety of our classroom community. It will stop. Now. We must move forward, and something must change before we do. I am certain that we can reach an immediate agreement about what that change needs to be. I'll help you. It does not feel like it right now, but we're in this together."

Once I've got my language down, I'm ready for my dress rehearsals. I can talk to kids about the things that tend to happen in the class: "Now that I really know us as a group, here are some things that I have noticed. . . ."

I like to take the opportunity of the dress rehearsal to talk to kids about the behavioral patterns that I have observed without shaming them or making them feel guilty, and I can talk about how I can help us as a team to be more productive and to have more fun.

> "Here are some things that I have planned for; whenever this happens, here is how I'm going to respond. I'm going to try some of those things out as we work in class today. Now that you know how I will respond to distractions, I want you to think about how you might respond to those same class distractions. Here are some options you can try. Let's chat about it at the end of class today."

This lets kids in on the reality that the job of a teacher is not to police or to catch them. The job of a teacher is to keep learning moving. In this paradigm, if kids are caught doing something, the message they perceive

Figure 4.8 *Ways to Respond to Disruptive Behaviors*

What I Say with My Voice	What I Say with My Body
Nothing—if I can change behavior without interrupting my lesson, this is the path that I want to take as often as possible.	I move to stand next to the person(s) who is the source of the behavior. I keep teaching. I squat to be eye level with the kid and make five to ten uncomfortable seconds of eye contact while I continue teaching my lesson. I stand and linger for ten more seconds while I keep teaching. When the behavior stops, I pause briefly to whisper my thanks to the kid, and I give him or her an affirming nod and a half smile before moving on.
Very little—if I must say something (and risk interrupting my lesson while drawing attention to disruptive behavior and to the kids involved), I want to make sure that my added distraction is as tiny as possible. For example: "[Name], please stop doing _____. Let's chat later about some things that you can do."	I move as close as possible to the person(s) involved, make eye contact, and whisper if possible.
Too much—if I have to talk for longer than ten seconds about disruptive student behavior, my response has now become an event, and I risk losing even more kids. For example, if three kids were involved in the initial disruption, and I stop class to talk about it, now thirty-two kids are involved. Can I postpone my response to the three and keep learning active for the twenty-nine? If so, that is the better option, as long as I make sure to address the three students sometime today. For example: "Hey, [name], we're all thinking about _____, and I want to give you an opportunity to think about it too. Check this out. . . ."	Because I run the risk of singling a student out, what I say here takes the focus away from the behavior itself and instead it extends a personal invitation for the kid to participate in a more productive way. Even though I'm probably a little annoyed by whatever this behavior is, my eyes and my body language cannot reveal this. Everything about my demeanor should say, "I want you in this lesson," because I do. I have to make sure that whatever comes next feels inclusive to that student. I might even include ad libs that affirm and continue to invite that specific student to participate as I continue my lesson.

is not "My teachers hate me"; the message is "I knew they were going to do that. Even if I don't like it, their response is mostly the same for everybody."

There are plenty of management techniques that can get kids to be quiet, to sit down, to turn in their work, and to stop saying unkind things. But even the most time-honored management strategies are at best temporary scaffolds that allow kids to reach the behavioral goals that we set for them. As such, management techniques leave kids dependent on us. When kids resist being managed, it can feel like they are resisting us as authority figures. Often what they are resisting is the feeling of being institutionalized.

They are right in their refusal. The approaches discussed here lead kids toward independence. Though it starts there, I don't want kids to be good just for me; I want them to be good for themselves. And for life.

"My job as a teacher is not to teach the curriculum or even to just teach the students; it is to seek to understand my kids as completely as possible so that I can purposefully bend curriculum to meet them."

5

Make Curriculum Work for *Your* Kids

When the curriculum is a problem:
"They said that I've got to do it this way."

I LOOKED AT THE SMILING CHILDREN ON THE FRONT OF THE BOOK.

"Look again," she commanded.

Mrs. Davenport was one of those teachers that everybody listened to. She'd earned it. I've met parents on back-to-school night who remembered when she taught them. They came, shuttling their children, the reverence from their days with her a generation ago still etched on their faces.

This was the same reverence etched on mine. She was authority and poise and intellect and high expectations personified. She was the living embodiment of the teacher look—the one that communicated love, inspired awe, and compelled you to listen.

Technically, I was her coach, but she spent her days *schooling* me. I heard every word.

"Look. Again. Cornelius." She enunciated every consonant sound in my name. As per usual, Mrs. Davenport did not come here to play.

I looked. The smiling kids on the front of the curriculum guide had not moved. I did not know what she wanted me to see. I did not tell her this. But my expression did.

She caressed my arm. Immediately I was at ease, but I was not off the hook. At all.

"These are not our children," she started.

All of a sudden, I saw what she wanted me to see. Of the faces smiling at me, none of them were Latinx, like our students. As far as we could tell, none of them seemed to be from Hungary or from China, like our students. None of them appeared to be West Indian, like our students. The lone African American student on the cover wore the uncomfortable expression of someone held against his will. In the scene depicted on the front of the book, his white classmates did not even notice. It was tragic. And comedic.

Mrs. Davenport spoke. "This book was given *to* us, but it was not written *for* us." This was not an observation. It was a verdict.

"Those people from the district plan for everything, Cornelius. You work with them sometimes. You know this."

I blinked—hard—in acknowledgment of this.

"It is very clear, even from the cover, young man, that they have not planned for us. So we are going to plan for us. We are going to take what they did, and build on it."

Mrs. Davenport was not asking. She was not sending an email for permission to alter the curriculum to the department or to the principal. And she certainly was not asking it of me. She was declaring. It was terrifyingly liberating.

Mrs. Davenport knew what I have come to value immensely. Any curriculum designed without her specific students in mind was not a curriculum that she was willing to use. What I've grown to understand about this refusal is that it is *not* an outright rejection of standard curriculum or the authority that wields it; rather it is a blanket admission that any curriculum or program that we buy, adopt, or create is incomplete until it includes our students and until it includes us.

Mrs. Davenport and the countless teachers like her have helped me to understand that my job as a teacher is not to teach the curriculum or even to just teach the students; it is to seek to understand my kids as completely as possible so that I can purposefully bend curriculum to meet them.

What we choose to teach can do great harm to children if we are not careful. Harmful curriculum is any curriculum that

- does not see students or the very specific lives that they lead
- is not flexible enough to be altered by the teachers who seek to use it, or
- does not educate or grow the practitioner.

Essentially, any curriculum that does not see my students cannot possibly be good for them. Any curriculum that is not flexible or malleable is not good for me. Any curriculum that does not teach me does not really aim to teach them.

I've realized that curriculum does not come out of the box like this. No curriculum—no matter how good—is ever going to see my kids. Not all programs want to help me be a better practitioner. Many just want to tell me what to do. It is up to me to change my curriculum to fit the needs of my students.

When the curriculum itself feels like it is the enemy, one way to eliminate this curricular hostility is to confront it, as Mrs. Davenport did, with your students in your heart and a pen in your hand.

Much has been written about what it means to make a curriculum that works for our kids. How do we even define who our kids are? And what does it mean that a curriculum works for them?

Where do I even start? For me the answer has been, "Not from scratch."

Crafting and sustaining an inclusive approach and pairing that with academic content takes insight and time and research and resources that I don't always have. Even if I had the resources to do so in a powerful way, spending my emotional and intellectual energy being fully present with kids would be a much smarter investment than spending that same energy simply preparing for them.

This does not mean that I eschew planning. This simply means that I'm smart about how I use my time.

I read the curriculum that I've been given or assigned or I start with a research base—someone else's. I look at research-based approaches that have been successful in other schools or classes, and I read what they did and how they did it. I consider the professional books that they read and the materials that they used or purchased.

Basically, I start where the people before me left off by learning as much as I can about my content and about what I am expected to do, what has been given to me, and what has worked in the past. This forms the foundation of my work by essentially giving me an original work to remix. I build on this foundation by getting to know my kids.

Before I know what to teach, I need to know whom I teach.

I've found that it's easy to take intellectual shortcuts when it comes to getting to know students. We've all met the kid that lives to please the teacher or the kid who exists to elude us. We've met the kids who do all of the things on time, and we've met the kids who don't seem to notice that there are things to be done. We seem to have these kids every year. With all of the work that we have to do each year, especially in the beginning when we are getting to know students, it can feel convenient to treat Jasmine, this year's teacher pleaser, just like last year's teacher pleaser, Rosa.

Such a stance is potentially dangerous because it erases kids and reduces them to a caricature or stereotype. In this paradigm, Jasmine never gets to be. She is silenced—stripped of identity—simply because she is seen as a variation of Rosa. Children can rarely ever name that this is happening to them, but they often feel it. And they definitely respond to it. This silencing and erasure happens disproportionately to children with disabilities and children of color.

Stereotypes abound in our work. We've all heard about the angry, poverty-stricken student and the lone charismatic teacher that helped him to achieve. Those tropes make for engaging cinema, but they make for horrible curriculum.

When I engage with the stereotypes of kids that I've been handed or with the caricatures that I've constructed, many kids will still respond positively. But this is a false positivity. It occurs largely because I am the teacher, and as such, I hold all of the power. A positive interaction based on a power imbalance—the powerful interacting with the powerless—is not a positive interaction. It is a colonizing one. We end up giving kids the things we think they need, not the things that will sustain their futures. No matter how well-intentioned we are when we do this, it is not teaching.

When I engage with the actual children in my class, this relationship forms the foundation for a curriculum that moves kids.

In relationships, it is the *process* of knowing that makes the dynamic powerful. What counts in any relationship is that the involved parties continue to invest in each other. In this regard, understanding or knowing our students is not something that we *achieve*. It is something that we *live*. Continually.

After studying the content itself, and beginning the labor to know the children that I want to serve, I typically end my work by making articulated and visible connections from the content to the kids' lived experiences and to their aspirations.

Before our kids are students, they are people. People care about other people; they care about ideas, trends, and experiences.

People want to learn more about things that they care about. They want to learn how those things came to be and they want to learn about the concepts that govern how those things operate in the world.

People want to discover new things that they can care about—things that will help them to dream beyond their current reality, things that can help them to thrive or to maintain or sometimes just to endure.

A curriculum without this kind of care is just a set of interrelated ideas that have failed in their most important relational aspect: the relationship that those ideas and activities have to kids and to their lives.

There was a time in my career when I felt like making those connections was magical. There were certain teachers on my team who were just perpetually hip. I, on the other hand, exhibited only periodic flashes of cool. I spent years searching for the magic.

On that quest I learned a few things:

- There is no magic. Knowing what kids care about and acting upon that knowledge can be learned.

- Classroom cool is not performative. It is relational. Most of this work happens when you are not "onstage."

- Many times we seek to foster a sense of compliance or one of accountability. Those things are based on us being powerful and kids being comparatively powerless. We can work instead to build trust. For kids, it's a more powerful place from which to learn.

> *"What counts in any relationship is that the involved parties continue to invest in each other."*

Laboring to know children and using our most audacious creativity to act on that knowing leave us with a curriculum that authentically seeks to teach and not just to instruct or to control. Additionally, an approach to curriculum that labors to see and to know kids for who they are and then acts on that knowing helps to grow us into sharper professionals. It broadens the concept of assessment to include not just knowing what people can do but knowing the people. It deepens our knowledge of content by helping us to become more flexible practitioners of what we teach, and it keeps the focus of our work on transference by ensuring that the things that we teach can be used by children to impact life beyond our classrooms.

Use a Universal-Design-for-Learning Framework to Make Learning Accessible

One of the first things I seek to know when I'm trying to figure out who my kids are is how they approach learning, and I want to make sure that whatever I'm doing feels accessible to those approaches. CAST's work has been so valuable in this area. Their work to remove barriers to learning has impacted my practice in a profound way.

Based on what I have learned from them, I use a universal-design-for-learning (UDL) framework, like the one in Figure 5.1, to think about how my students approach learning. I try to be as inclusive as I can in all of my teaching, but I lean on the methods and approaches to which students respond most favorably. I want to notice general trends, and I want to pay attention to outliers. My work must include approaches that are accessible to all students.

In Figure 5.2 I share some things you can try in each category. When you are planning from a curriculum that you have been given, all of these are deliberate things to do inside of it to give kids greater access to the learning.

Remember, as you try each of these things, there is no universally amazing practice. There is no such thing as *the* way to deliver a lecture

Figure 5.1 *One Way to Think About a Universal-Design-for-Learning Framework*

How does this child seem to respond when I . . .

. . . consider different ways that the information I present can be represented?

- Use different media, symbols, or languages.
- Present information nonverbally.
- Give background information to guide thinking.

. . . create different opportunities for action and expression in the classroom?

- Have tools available for them to express themselves beyond writing and speaking.
- Encourage movement and performance.
- Provide supports so that students can come up with their own planning and organizational systems.

. . . foster multiple ways to sustain engagement?

- Offer choice and options that feel valuable and relevant to children.
- Create opportunities for authentic feedback and collaboration.
- Make time and space for kids to work through frustration, confusion, or mistakes.

or to introduce a concept. There is a way that works for some of your students, and *another* way that works for them, and this *other* way that seems to work for them when the postlunch weirdness sets in.

When you dive into this work, if you do so looking for solutions, you will come up empty-handed. Though our kids might face challenges, they are not problems to solve. Begin, instead, by looking for possibility. You will find that some things work in particular contexts or with particular kids but not with others. Our work with young people has always been about trial and error. The best teachers recognize that errors—even the

Figure 5.2 *Some Things to Try Within the Universal-Design-for-Learning Framework*

How can you consider different ways that the information you present can be represented?	**Use different media, symbols, or languages.** ☐ Try to support your lecture with photographs that enhance the content. ☐ Use audio or video to allow kids to practice skills that you hope they will use in traditional texts. ☐ Translate charts or visuals into other languages (including some nonstandard forms of English) to allow kids to use them more independently. ☐ Other:
	Present information nonverbally. ☐ Use facial expressions and gestures to communicate meaning as you read to and talk with kids. ☐ Illustrate charts with simple pictures and icons that communicate meaning. Use color. ☐ Show pictures of what it looks like to be doing the thing that you want children to do. Use props, tools, or manipulatives in demonstrations. Allow kids to do the same. ☐ Other:
	Give background information to guide thinking. ☐ If there is any information that kids need to be able to engage in a lesson, give that information the day before. Use charts, children's books, media, or games on the topic. Allow them to revisit these things as needed. Don't expect that they know it. ☐ Demonstrate what it is like to think through a problem or concept and make sure that kids have access to those ways of thinking through charts, partners, exemplar videos, or other tools. ☐ Allow kids to invent tools and processes that support their thinking and their work. Acknowledge that they don't have to do it the teacher way; rather, they just need a way that works for them. ☐ Other:

Figure 5.2 *Some Things to Try Within the Universal-Design-for-Learning Framework* (continued)

How can you create different opportunities for action and expression in the classroom?	**Have tools available for them to express themselves beyond writing and speaking.** ☐ Create a supply area that you reference during lessons. Show kids how they can choose to do a task with pens, markers, different types of paper, any available technology, or in a way that works optimally for them. ☐ Make time for rehearsals before work time, so that kids can practice how their work might go. Encourage them to rehearse dealing with difficulty or working through challenges, and then champion this work when they do it independently. ☐ Talk to children about how they work best, and help them to think about tools to translate their preferred methods of expression into other forms. ☐ Other:
	Encourage movement and performance. ☐ Make opportunities for kids to act out ideas and concepts so they feel more tangible and concrete to them. ☐ Allow for purposeful movement breaks. ☐ Different parts of the lesson can happen in different parts of the classroom. This allows kids to move in predictable ways across the day. ☐ Other:
	Provide supports so that students can come up with their own planning and organizational systems. ☐ Give kids the schedule at the beginning of the day or period. Build in places where they can choose how the time will be spent. Give them options and teach them how to assign priority to tasks and occurrences. ☐ When sharing directions, don't demonstrate just one way that a thing can be done. Show several ways. Invite students to choose or to make up their own ways. ☐ Think out loud about supplies and resources—how they are distributed, shared, used, and stored. Give students time to consider their own logistics. ☐ Other:

continues

Figure 5.2 *Some Things to Try Within the Universal-Design-for-Learning Framework* (continued)

How can you foster multiple ways to sustain engagement?	**Offer choice and options that feel valuable and relevant to children.** ☐ Allow opportunities for students to think about things that they are already good at and transfer the skills associated with those things to something they are not good at yet. ☐ Demonstrate how the in-class learning is directly connected to things that are important in kids' lives. ☐ Allow kids opportunities to use their skills to examine or solve problems that are meaningful to them. ☐ Other:
	Create opportunities for authentic feedback and collaboration. ☐ Establish partnerships and teach students how to work collaboratively. Relationships take work, so expect students to make mistakes. Allow them to work on low-stakes tasks together in preparation for higher-stakes collaborations later. ☐ Talk to kids periodically about their work, and show them (demonstrate; don't tell) specific ways that they can make it better. ☐ Allow kids to determine who the audience for their work will be. How can they use their developing skills to do work that might benefit or make an impression on friends or community members? ☐ Other:
	Make time and space for kids to work through frustration, confusion, or mistakes. ☐ Expect mistakes and plan for them. Help kids to understand that you welcome mistakes by demonstrating how to work through them and how to learn from them. ☐ When kids try to do things one way and it does not work for them, help them understand that there are other ways to do the thing. Not everyone must do the thing in the same uniform way. ☐ Ask kids what tools they will need to make their work easier, and create the time in class to co-construct those tools. Allow kids to practice using them. ☐ Other:

public ones that can feel embarrassing or disastrous—are opportunities to reflect (teacher happy hour?), to make adjustments, and to try again.

When we get assigned a curriculum or an approach, many of us are made to feel that we've got to stick to the script, or teach the thing as is. This is not true.

The script, schedule, or plan that you have been handed exists as a blueprint that was crafted in someone else's classroom, for their students. To make it work for your kids, you must consider them.

If the plan suggests a lecture, you've got to consider your children. Is a lecture good for them, or do they need a lecture with visuals? Or a lecture with opportunities to process the information verbally? Or a lecture with gestures and opportunities to move?

The work of asking these questions and aggressively pursuing possible answers is not deviating from the curriculum. You are moving closer to it by making sure that it has the features that will allow your students to access and understand it.

Understand Exactly What You're Being Asked to Do

A few years ago, my grade team was asked to do a close read of Martin Luther King Jr.'s "Letter from Birmingham Jail" with all of the seventh-grade students at school. I was beyond excited. King's letter is one of my favorite texts on the planet. I read it as a teen, and to this day it continues to shape my work and worldview. It is one of the most important things ever written.

I thought about my students and about how that letter offers an active hope, not just warm feelings. King lays out a blueprint for action, service, and principled disobedience that is so relevant and needed today. He explains his relationship to the law, reframes what it means to value justice, and expresses anger at those who obstruct it. My students needed this (so do yours).

I also thought about their reading ability, about the strength of their focus when navigating challenging texts, and about how to best engage them in such an important work.

And then I looked at the lesson plan that I had been handed: "Read the text. Underline key words. Answer the questions."

The lesson plan tried to turn my hero into a worksheet. King's radical urgency was reduced to a multiple-choice question and two fill-in-the-blank sentences.

Nope. Not today. Not ever.

But here was my challenge: I had to do what my literacy coach suggested. I couldn't skip this lesson. And it was King. I wouldn't *want* to skip this lesson. But I couldn't do Martin Luther King fill-in-the-blank activities. It felt cheap.

Because I understood my kids, I had to turn this lesson into something they could access and learn from. So I thought through this.

What was I being asked to do?

This lesson seemed to value close reading. It wanted kids to use this strategy to arrive at a deeper understanding of Martin Luther King. I was good with that.

Why close reading?

If I could get kids to do this in a meaningful way, it would help them to see more in other texts, in other people, and in the world. I was good with that too. Though I'm not sure everyone in my department saw this as I did. Some people were viewing the request to do this as just another activity.

I understand where this sentiment came from. There is so much to do in a school. Often when we are asked to do things, those asks come without context or depth because we've got to pick the kids up from lunch or drop them off at music. Conversations that should be thoughtful ones end up being had in hallways, over the heads of animated children, as we pass by the colleagues that we have been meaning to see. In an ideal world, we would have talked about why the Birmingham letter is important to read with children. But because the superintendent would be visiting next week and the book fair needed three more volunteers, Martin Luther King Jr. became another thing we had to do.

> *"The lesson plan tried to turn my hero into a worksheet . . . radical urgency was reduced to a multiple-choice question and two fill-in-the-blank sentences."*

One way to fight bad curriculum is simply to slow down. To be choosy. To prioritize the things that really matter. What really mattered in this case was that kids got practice exploring how rich texts can be.

Once we're clear on what matters, a whole range of options opens up. Was there another way to do this?

There was. Several, in fact. This did not have to be "Read the text. Underline key words. Answer the questions," like I'd been told. This could be deeper, richer. The lesson that I'd been handed was a foundation. It did not have to be the entire structure.

As much as I love King's letter, I didn't even have to start this experience with it. I could have had kids start by exploring the richness of texts that were familiar to them as a way for them to practice their reading moves before we shifted our attention to examining King. That way they wouldn't be using new reading strategies at the same time as they were being introduced to King's powerful prose. We could handle one thing at a time.

First, we'd get used to new reading strategies.

Then we'd use these strategies to read an incredibly complex and richly rewarding text.

This reworking of my coach's request was not a refusal to teach the curriculum. It was a deeper look at the curriculum. An exploration of what it really aimed to do, my students' capacity to access it, and my ability as a practitioner to deliver it. It was a refusal to teach the curriculum in a way that would not see children and that would not value me or my professional growth.

This type of work can be done alone, but it is better done in pairs or teams. I can invite a colleague to sit and think through something with me or we can talk it out on the phone. I've spent years of my career talking about the things that are wrong. This kind of constructive talk repositions us. We are not victims in a dysfunctional system; we are agents with the vision to imagine new systems—even if they exist only in our individual classrooms or departments for now.

Any time I am given a curriculum or lessons to teach, I need to know exactly what I am being asked to do. I use the questions in Figure 5.3 to think through what I've been given so that I can use it as an effective foundation for my teaching. This deeper look at curriculum can look like

"One way to fight bad curriculum is to simply to slow down. . . . To prioritize the things that really matter."

Sample Questions That Help Me Understand What I'm Being Asked to Teach

	What, exactly, am I being asked to do? (Sometimes the thing will have many parts. Try to name all of the parts below.)		
	1.	2.	3.
Things that the lesson or curriculum that I've been given is asking me to do			
Why is this thing important? ("Because it's for a test" or "Because the curriculum says so" does not count.) What will students actually learn? How is this learning valuable?			
There is more than one way to do this. How might I try to do this thing in my classroom to make it work? (These are not solutions; they are simply ideas. Doing the thing as is is an option too!)			

	1.	2.	3.
What tools will I need to make to support the students as they try this work? (This requires a bit of creativity. You can also ask the kids!) Will they need the tools forever or will I teach kids to outgrow them or create their own tools?			
Kids will not master anything instantly, so how will I know if I am being successful?			
What have I learned about myself, my students, or my practice that I can save and use later?			

Figure 5.3 *Questions That Help Me Understand What I'm Being Asked to Teach*

this. Even if you cannot think through or answer all of these questions, engaging in this work can turn any mandate into a much richer experience for your students and a much richer experience for you.

Questions That Help Me Understand What I'm Being Asked to Teach (Online Resource 5.1) can be found with the Companion Resources.

Figure 5.4 shows what it can look like when I use the questions to think about something I've been told to do with my class.

This kind of creative thinking is the part of teaching that is an art. We decided that instead of starting with King's letter right away, we would work with more familiar texts as practice and then move into King. This did not come from a lesson plan book. No one told us to do this. We considered what we knew about our students and what we knew from our professional learning and we decided this. We created these conditions. We added the extra step because it was good for children. Art.

Figure 5.4 *Questions That Help Me Understand What I'm Being Asked to Teach Sample*

Sample Questions That Help Me Understand What I'm Being Asked to Teach

What, exactly, am I being asked to do? (Sometimes the thing will have many parts. Try to name all of the parts below.)			
I've been asked to assign Martin Luther King Jr.'s "Letter from Birmingham Jail" to students. They are to read the text, underline key words, and answer the questions.			
Things that the lesson or curriculum that I've been given is asking me to do.	1. This assignment seems to value close reading. It wants kids to have a deep understanding of this letter.	2. This assignment also seems to value vocabulary. It wants kids to understand King's language.	3. This assignment values the significance of King himself. Kids should know why he's important.
Why is this thing important? ("Because it's for a test" or "Because the curriculum says so" does not count.) What will students actually learn? How is this learning valuable?	The close reading that they want kids to do here can serve them well in other texts. If I teach this well, this can help them to navigate difficulty or get more out of what they read.	This can prove to be a great study of how word choice gives a writer a personal style. They can sharpen their craft by studying King's.	This is an introduction to King beyond the sound bites. Today's sound-bite culture robs kids of nuanced heroes. We are nuanced. As King was. This is important to learn.
There is more than one way to do this. How might I try to do this thing in my classroom to make it work? (These are not solutions; they are simply ideas. Doing the thing as is is an option too!)	Instead of just assigning this ("Read this. Answer the questions"), I can model effective close reading on this or another text so that kids understand both the strategy and the text.	I could have them listen to audio of King's other work to get a sense of his cadence and style. We can look for patterns and then check to see if we see the same trends in the Birmingham letter.	We can think about how King uses the letter to position himself, his peers, and his cause. We can think about how to engage in that work ourselves.

continues

Figure 5.4 *Questions That Help Me Understand What I'm Being Asked to Teach Sample* (continued)

	1.	2.	3.
What tools will I need to make to support the students as they try this work? (This requires a bit of creativity. You can also ask the kids!) Will they need the tools forever or will I teach kids to outgrow them or create their own tools?	If kids are doing this kind of close reading for the first time, I will want to start them on a more accessible text or media to practice their close reading moves before attempting to tackle King's prose. I could have kids think about questions to always ask of a text.	I can make word cards or add to a word wall. Or I can play some vocabulary games to get them to think actively about these terms. I might even have them make models of specific words. Or match words to historical images from that time.	Children don't think often enough about how to position themselves in a social ecosystem. They often feel like they earn their reputations by chance. I could build some opportunities for role-playing and reflection that would force kids to think about how one intentionally builds a persona. We could plan for the personas they want to build and search for the words they will use as tools.
Kids will not master anything instantly, so how will I know if I am being successful?	I'll know that I'm being successful when kids start to move beyond summary into interpretation. This can look any number of ways, but I'll be listening for a few tells, including "I think" and "because" and "I wonder."	I'll know that they are moving forward when I see them playing around with words—even if they use them wrong. I should probably create low-stakes opportunities for them to play with words.	This can start a conversation about how we want to be remembered. I'll know that I'm moving toward success when kids are actively thinking about the relationship among their words and their actions. I can look for traces of success all over the school day.
What have I learned about myself, my students, or my practice that I can save and use later?	This can help me to get good at facilitating close reading activities. Also this really helps me to consider the difference between teaching and merely assigning. I've taken this assignment and turned it into real teaching.	This helps me to consider that kids can approximate. Learning is messy. My goal is not to get them to use words perfectly here. My goal is to get them to be comfortable enough to not fear trying new words in classroom contexts.	I can think more about the kind of people that kids become after doing my classwork, and I can make specific in-class comments about how the things that we study allow them to lead better lives *right now*, not years from now. This is important.

Understand What Test Prep Is Really Asking You to Do

We can be similarly artful when it comes to preparing for standardized tests and other exams. I use the same chart to think through the kind of test preparation that I am often asked to do with children.

So much of our time, energy, and resources are spent preparing kids for tests. As teachers we are in quite the predicament when it comes to testing.

Much of what is peddled to us as test prep is not authentic learning. But many of our students are compliantly conditioned to it. This is complicated by the reality that for many of us, our schools, our funding, and our jobs depend on kids doing well on these exams.

It has been well documented that standardization, assessment, and measurement are not bad things at all. But an unhealthy emphasis on any of these things can be detrimental to a learning community and harmful to children.

Each testing season, my disdain springs anew for what the testing industrial complex has done to our profession, to our schools, and to our children. We exist in a world where some kids know their scores and levels more intimately than they know their reading interests.

But I am also loyal to a community that has been plagued by school closures, and I am dedicated to doing my part to keep them open. I am committed to its children, who are often overlooked because of their zip code. I know that opportunity will ignore those five numbers if they are attached to an attractive reading score. I know that this isn't right, but I also know that this is the game, and that children, their parents, and I must play it. Well. Until we can smash it to pieces and build another one—one that sees them, beyond the neighborhood and beyond their parents' income, for the beautiful humans that they are.

Until then, I've got to be good at helping to build three-dimensional humans who can learn all the literacy, math, science, history, and love that I can teach and apply those skills in the classroom, in the community, and in the cold and sometimes hostile context of periodic tests.

This is essential work, and it can be done by asking the same questions. Start with the most important one: When I am being handed test-prep materials, what, really, am I being asked to do?

Simple. I'm being asked to teach children how to do the things that I have already taught them how to do—calculating fractions, understanding ionic bonding, explaining the causes of multinational conflict, interpreting a text—in the very specific context of a standardized test.

Test prep is not about teaching kids some new thing so that they can pass a test. Rather, authentic test prep says, "I've already taught you this thing. Allow me to teach you the layout of the test and how you can apply the thing that you already know to this new terrain." It is important to understand that test prep is not teaching. It is transference. Figure 5.5 shows what it can look like when I use the questions to think about test prep.

Thinking about curriculum or about standardized testing through the lenses of access, choice, flexibility, and my own professional learning helps me to design curriculum that works specifically for the children in front of me.

In this way we can create tools that kids might need. We can help kids to use those tools.

In this way we can read curriculum with a lens of student proficiency, not just one of student or teacher compliance.

In this way we can decide what we need to learn to meet the dynamic needs of our students, we can put ourselves in position to learn those things, and we can forgive ourselves as we make the mistakes essential to this kind of growth.

In this way we are artists.

In this way we are free.

And we cannot expect to raise free thinkers if we are not demonstratively free ourselves.

As it is now, so much of contemporary teaching is waiting for someone to tell us what to do. It does not have to be that way. We can create a thing, try it, reflect on it, and change it. This ability to read a room of children, create a thing for them, recognize when the thing isn't working for the children, and alter or change the thing completely is the most underdeveloped set of teacher skills. We cannot purchase our way into this. This requires time and study and practice. This is listening to what kids need. This is assessment. This is data analysis. This is intervention.

This is you.

Figure 5.5 *Questions That Help Me Understand What I'm Being Asked to Teach—Test-Prep Sample*

Sample Questions That Help Me Understand What I'm Being Asked to Teach

What, exactly, am I being asked to do? (Sometimes the thing will have many parts. Try to name all of the parts below.)				
I'm being asked to help kids use skills they've already practiced in the context of a standardized test.				
Things that the lesson or curriculum that I've been given is asking me to do	1. Give kids authentic practice at using existing skills.	2. Teach kids how and when to apply those skills to new situations.	3. Teach kids how the tests go, so that the new terrain of the assessment has no surprises.	4. Create opportunities for kids to make tools, strategies, and approaches that work for them in this new terrain.
Why is this thing important? ("Because it's for a test" or "Because the curriculum says so" does not count.) What will students actually learn? How is this learning valuable?	Sometimes kids learn how to do a thing only in the context that we taught it in. Authentic practice lets kids try strategies in new contexts, in new circumstances, and under different conditions. This is essential for learning.	We spend much of our time teaching kids what or how. We don't talk often enough about when, and there is rarely ever enough time to practice this kind of decision making.	Teaching kids how to prepare for a test by studying its structure and tendencies is an important life skill. We want kids to prepare for job interviews, colleges, doctors, and housing opportunities by studying. That work can start in the classroom.	In school, we rely too heavily on telling kids what strategies might work for them. It is important to allow kids to experiment with skill use. This allows them to invent strategies that can work for them.
There is more than one way to do this. How might I try to do this thing in my classroom to make it work? (These are not solutions; they are simply ideas. Doing the thing as is is an option too!)	Kids can practice skills by talking through problems, making things, reading texts, testing hypotheses, role-playing, or visiting a place. Any application of the skills that they have learned is effective preparation for using those skills on a test.	We can look at different kinds of challenges and consider all that we know and what we might select from that repertoire to approach those challenges. This can be gamified and applied to everyday tasks like organizing art supplies or collecting papers or it can be done through talk or writing for more academic tasks.	Kids can look at old tests to notice patterns I can take them on a tour through practice materials and help familiarize them with the language and structure of the test. Kids can discuss the best approaches for each section. These can be compiled, posted in the room, and reviewed often before practice sessions.	As children practice, they can renegotiate their skill and strategy repertoires by naming the strategies that work best for tests and retiring the ones that don't. These will be personal lists, and they will vary from kid to kid, but this activity will leave kids feeling ready—armed with things that they helped to invent.

continues

Figure 5.5 *Questions That Help Me Understand What I'm Being Asked to Teach—Test-Prep Sample* (continued)

	1.	2.	3.	4.
Kids will not master anything instantly, so how will I know if I am being successful?	I'll know that I'm successful when I see kids using skills I taught beyond the content that I taught it in. This means that I have to create opportunities that feel flexible enough for kids to experiment and improvise. My assessment must look for and privilege that improvisation.	I'll know that I'm successful when kids are considering the skills in their personal repertoire . . . when they can explain how they did a thing and why they did it that way. Again, I must create opportunities for this to happen in the classroom, and I'll have to model how it is done.	I'll know that I'm successful when thinking about how their skills might work in a testing (or any other) context feels normal to them, when in preparation, they talk about approaching the exam like they talk about approaching a video game: "The first part of it goes like this, so I could do it this way . . . or it could work if I try it like this . . ."	I'll know that I'm successful when kids grow increasingly comfortable with using tools that we co-construct to approach the exam.
What have I learned about myself, my students, or my practice that I can save and use later?	The big takeaways from any time spent preparing kids for standardized exams should be the things that I learn about transference and independence. Two questions that I should always be grappling with as a practitioner are 1. How do I work to teach kids how to do a skill in multiple contexts, and then how do I create the time to make sure that they practice this often? 2. How do I create space for kids to think about the ways that work best for them to think and to work? Are their ways of doing and knowing valued in my classroom?			

Loving kids and loving teaching and loving your content are powerful. You are already that. We don't need heroes. Being able to wield assessment, analysis, and intervention in ways that speak to what children need is transformative. We can study and practice our way into this. Our children need us to be powerful. Our future needs us to be transformative.

"Though our culture celebrates innovation, at times it encourages and rewards compliance. When we look across our schools, it can seem that the people who move forward are the ones whose loyalty to mandate outlasts their bonds to creativity. We talk about entrepreneurial spirit while worshipping at the altar of status quo."

Being a Good Teacher Versus Being a Good Employee

"They told me to be an innovator right before they handed me a list of twenty-three nonnegotiable items."

THERE IS AN ACKNOWLEDGMENT IN ALL COMICS THAT THE reader is intelligent. In the act of storytelling, there is an inherent respect offered. Storytellers assume goodwill, competence, curiosity, and tenacity.

A good storyteller does not ask you to love the characters, because they know that if they do their jobs, you will. Those who conjure stories understand that you will follow the adventure—no matter how complex—because they know that you can. It is expected that you will question things and that you won't give up, even if the protagonist does.

When experiencing stories, readers, listeners, and viewers pick up on this. It's part of what makes these stories easy to love. Additionally, we love hero stories because we get to see our icons overcome danger in the form of rampant fear, oppression, and injustice.

Along with our love, one understanding that we bring with us into these stories is that when dealing with such danger, the potential for death is real.

In the hero books and movies, death is an uncredited actor. People flirt with it and they challenge it. Above all, our culture celebrates heroes because those that we cheer for spend much of their time evading it.

Be it through guile, superpower, miraculous circumstance, time travel, cloning, or good old-fashioned resurrection, our heroes are never out of the picture for too long. The heroes personified in our contemporary myths tend to be a type. To many of them, death is simply a cliché. We've seen Superman reborn, seen Wolverine regenerate, and watched parallel universes consolidate to allow characters like Flash and Peter Parker to persist.

As educators, we, too, tend to be a type. Many of us became passionate about education because we ourselves had positive school experiences. Most of us earned our success by being the smart ones, the ones with our hands up, the ones who listened, did the homework, or organized the group project. In public, we were the rule followers—the compliant ones.

That nature has not left us.

When merit or social standing is at stake, and we are asked to do a thing, we tend to be the kind of people that do the thing. As asked.

This becomes difficult and potentially paralyzing in contexts like teaching, where we are asked to do things that might not be universally good for all children.

I know that curriculum simply suggests what I should teach. I know that it does not dictate the how and that it certainly cannot mandate the why. I know all of this, but I'm a natural rule follower. I want to be liked by the principal. I want to be the one that gets the commendation for doing a good job. If there's a rubric, I want to be "highly effective."

And sometimes I'm not sure if the principal or the teaching rubric sees teaching practice that is *becoming*. I've begun to fear that it sees only practice that is a perfect reflection of what it asked for. Much of my teacher stress is born in the liminal space between taking calculated risks to grow my practice in service of kids and doing what the boss told me to do.

How do I negotiate that? Especially when teacher evaluation—*my* evaluation—is at stake?

Though our culture celebrates innovation, at times it encourages and rewards compliance. When we look across our schools, it can seem that the people who move forward are the ones whose loyalty to mandate outlasts their bonds to creativity. We talk about entrepreneurial spirit while worshipping at the altar of status quo.

This can be frustrating and potentially paralyzing, especially when the way forward requires us to move in innovative ways in order to serve our students. So much of our educator energy can be burned by simply navigating change that we've got little effort left to actually be change.

What happens when there is no mandate or script illuminating the path forward? Where does my innovation live on the rubric for effective teaching?

In short, it lives at the top.

And with some effort, we can help the people around us to understand that.

As her thinking has evolved, Gloria Ladson-Billings has reminded us that as educators, "if we stop growing, we will die, and, more importantly, our students will wither and die in our presence" (2014, 77).[1] She calls this a sort of "classroom death," adding that "death in the classroom refers to teachers who stop trying to reach each and every student or teachers that succumb to rules and regulations that are dehumanizing [to students] and result in de-skilling" (Apple 1993).[2]

We lament student disengagement or failure; these are the chief by-products of this "death."

Ladson-Billings is absolutely right. Yet I think about all the instances—when I have been tired, outmatched, or overwhelmed—when, according to her definition, I have chosen death. Willingly.

Given the huge investment required to work as we must, what can it mean to truly live as Ladson-Billings suggests? And for those of us who have embraced death before, is there such a thing as resurrection?

The stories that we consume would suggest that there is.

Cheating Death

To grow under the authoritatively well-intentioned eyes of principals and districts can feel like a complicated dance. I've got to embrace the unknown by engaging in professional study and then try new things that

---

1. Ladson-Billings, Gloria. 2014. "Culturally Relevant Pedagogy 2.0: A.K.A. the Remix." *Harvard Educational Review* 84 (1): 74–84.

2. Apple, Michael W. 1993. "The Politics of Official Knowledge: Does a National Curriculum Make Sense?" *Teachers College Record* 95 (2): 222–41.

I won't immediately be good at, all while looking like I know what I'm doing so as not to draw negative attention to myself or to my public imperfections.

Some of us are fortunate to work in places where we are expected to learn in public or where the community value is on growth rather than "gotcha"—in these places, this dance is not necessary.

In some schools and departments, however, attention means that there will be people in my room giving me advice to which I'll be account-able. If I am lucky, that advice will take into account the kind of growth that my kids need me to make and push me in that direction. If I am unlucky, that advice will dogmatically remind me to stick to the script, program, or mandate. These moments are not just stressful and scary; they are the moments when I am most likely to choose apathy, resigned compliance, or rote implementation—Ladson-Billings' classroom death.

But we can live as she suggests while doing this dance well, and it does not involve hiding in our classrooms and doing the work in covert isolation. There is certainly a time for this kind of subversive progress, but that time cannot be always. Staying in my room with the door closed is a certain path to stagnation and burnout.

When it feels like you don't have the institutional freedom to grow like you want to, you actually do.

Though I wish it could be, planning one's own growth is not as simple as choosing a smart technique and trying it. There are times when you will have to be strategic about how you move forward.

This work is equal parts mind-set, communication, and classroom execution. Figure 6.1 shows an overview of what the process of planning your own teacher growth can look like.

The steps in this process do not flow in a linear order, but when plan-ning for how I want to grow to be better for children, I tend to start with mind-set. For me, the hardest work is always on my own attitude about the work at hand, so I start there.

Engage in Imaginative Mind-Set Work

There are so many times at school when we believe that nothing will change. Though some may see it as such, this is not being nega-tive. Many of our beliefs that things will never change are built upon

Figure 6.1 *Process of Planning Your Own Teacher Growth*

Imaginative Mind-Set Work	Communication	In-Classroom Work
Believe that things can be different. Acknowledge that things might not change in the way that you want them to change. Read and study widely to search for ideas of what to try.	Set goals. Communicate your goals and the benchmarks that you hope to meet on the way to those goals. Invite students and adults to give you feedback, but give yourself feedback first.	Try out what you learn. Invite a friend to join you. Reflect on your teaching practice so you can make small adjustments that allow the work to move forward productively.

experience. You know your building; you know your colleagues; you know how things tend to go. It is important here to acknowledge the traditions, limitations, and patterns that you know to be true, but it is more important to begin to imagine the new realities that can be true.

When we want to be self-determining in terms of our professional growth, the first thing that we can do is believe that things can be different. We certainly cannot expect to change an entire school or even a classroom yet, but we can change how we respond to the things that happen in those places.

This response and the kind of imaginative work that we can choose to do after it is at the center of any freedom struggle. Specifically, imagination will be central to the work of being free to grow in the ways that can most powerfully serve our students.

Whenever I find myself complaining or gossiping about a thing, I know that it's time to do some growing. I understand that the stories that I tell at the teacher happy hour—the "Can you believe that?!" ones—are coping strategies, not change mechanisms.

These stories, and the valid complaints that they personify, allow me to laugh, cry, or shrug my way through the impossible things that happen daily. They allow me to cope. They do not make the impossible situation possible. But they can. A lot of the stories that could potentially lead to change get left at the bar or in the teachers' lounge or in the tear-stained box of tissues in my best friend's classroom.

Each of the stories that we tell about our work, no matter how we embellish or downplay it, communicates some truth about the realities that we live. Taken collectively, those stories point to the persisting issues and to the school power structures that can plague us. And they shed some light on how we can work on ourselves so that we may better survive these things and develop the power to eventually change them altogether.

As I imagine change in the context of my own work, I sometimes have to fight the urge to say, "That's impossible," or "They won't let me do that." You'll have to do the same. Remember that to many of our heroes, freedom from bondage, full suffrage, and complete citizenship were impossible dreams too.

When impossibility keeps surfacing, one way to push past it is by saying, "What if?"

What if I could change the way that the kids entered the room? What if I could allow for more choice? What if I could engage kids differently? What if I had more time to take care of myself? Imagine what that would look and feel like, and assume, for now, that it is possible.

Once you've practiced seeing beyond the ceilings that we sometimes put on our own work, Figure 6.2 shows one way that your strategic imagination can work.

A blank version of the Tool to Engage in Imaginative Mind-Set Work (Online Resource 6.1) can be found with the Companion Resources.

Once I have started this imaginative mind-set work by considering my stories, I continue it by considering the actual work. I get to build the thing of my dreams. Here's the thing about this, though: the thing in our dreams—that thing that we want for our classroom or our students or our community or ourselves—exists in our mind in a state of imagined perfection.

As educators, sometimes we fail to act on our dreams because we fear that we cannot attain the perfection that we imagine. In truth, we won't find this perfection right away. Dream work is messy, but when faced with the choice between the sometimes broken reality of what currently exists and the messy reality of progress, it is better to live in the mess.

If we choose to act, things can be different. They won't be radically different right away, but they can be incrementally better.

The longer I stay in it, the more I realize that our work is more evolutionary than it is revolutionary.

I always have to remind myself here that I am not the first educator to ever struggle. I'm not the first one to dream of better, and I'm not the first one to try to imagine tomorrows that are slightly better than our todays. As such, when I'm thinking about things that I can do or approaches that I can take to solve my problems or work through my challenges, I can lean on the experience of others as presented in books, articles, conversations, or virtual interactions. I can learn from their mistakes and stand on a foundation of their successes.

When engaging in this kind of learning, it is important to do so authentically by remembering that we are doing this kind of thinking to free ourselves. We are not running from one orthodoxy to the next. This is not the work of questioning the methods of the leaders at school only to embrace the methods of random people on the Internet.

This is the work of questioning everything and building paths for ourselves and our students based on our own study, consideration, planning, and trial and error, not on someone else's promises of shortcuts and miracles.

When I consume professional materials, I do so with my students in mind always. Unless the person whose advice I'm following personally knows my students, I ask the questions in Figure 6.3.

Once I learn how to listen to advice, this impacts how I attend professional development, how I read professional texts, and how I surf the Internet. When you read, listen, think, and question powerfully, you'll find that you are all the expert that you'll ever need.

Gather a PR Team as You Make a Plan to Be Better for Kids

Once I've done some imaginative mind-set work and searched for ideas of what to try, I can set goals and communicate them.

I like to start by naming my goal in specific terms, like, "I want to create better systems to serve Marcus," or "I want to prioritize tasks that

Figure 6.2 *Tool to Engage in Imaginative Mind-Set Work*

What are the stories that I tell when I talk about my teaching?	I feel silenced by a few other members of the grade team. I'm decently well liked, but I'm definitely not in the club. Sometimes they make decisions without me or dismiss ideas that I have. It's not mean or unkind, but it happens regularly enough for me to know when it's coming. I joke about it, because sometimes that's all that I can do.	Marcus will not stop disrupting class. Sometimes it is good-natured and humorous, but most times it is just annoying because it happens so consistently. I have to respond to him so regularly that it feels like dealing with Marcus is in my job description. Some mornings when I don't feel like coming to school, it's because I fear dealing with the random situations that I know he will introduce. This is not a healthy thought, but I still think it.	Sometimes I'm so over-whelmed with planning and grading and simply being that I feel anxious. Most often it is insomnia, but sometimes I can't eat or I just want to be alone. Most evenings, when I get home, I am too tired to work, so I end up just thinking about it all night. This can sometimes keep me from enjoying the things that I should be enjoying.
What are the issues here?	Maybe people on the team think that I don't have much to offer. Maybe they are used to doing things the same way. Maybe my ideas seem impossible to them. Maybe I have not paid my dues. Maybe I'm not communicating my ideas in a way that allows them to hear me as I wish to be heard.	I don't want to think it, but maybe Marcus does not find my lessons relevant or engaging. Maybe I can work on learning more about him, building a relationship. Maybe Marcus can't access my lessons as I teach them. Maybe Marcus feels powerless, and this is how he becomes powerful. Maybe there is something else going on with Marcus that is forcing this behavior. Maybe all of these things are happening at once.	Maybe I need to ask for help. Perhaps I'm not organized enough to do all of this at once. I definitely need to let some things go (and to practice saying no). I could work on prioritizing and time management. Of course, I need more sleep and exercise.

Are there any major themes here?	▪ Work goes better when there is trust and collaboration.		
	▪ People can be more receptive to me when I am clear about the contributions that I intend to make.		
	▪ I can organize my work around what kids need, and I can use my documented in-classroom experience to explain that need.		
	▪ School goes best when kids feel powerful. To create the conditions for kids to be empowered, I need to consider choice, relevance, access, and engagement.		
	▪ In school there is no singular cause for a given thing. Things don't occur in black-and-white, this-or-that binaries. Sometimes educators can learn to be comfortable in the gray. When working through a challenge, I can explore multiple options, at once even.		
	▪ At work, it is OK to ask for help and direction.		
	▪ When educating children, it is OK to say no. We cannot expect ourselves to do everything.		
What are the common people, policies, and situations involved in my issues?	▪ Common people: the members of my grade team, Marcus, me		
	▪ Common policies: the reading curriculum, the classroom rules, lesson-planning guidelines		
	▪ Common situations: in-class disruptions, team meetings, lesson planning at home		
What are some things that I can do in the short term to deal with things as they are?	I can work on communicating clearly with the grade team, being clear about the kinds of support that I'll need from them and about the ways that I have and will continue to contribute.	Because I know Marcus' patterns, I can create some go-to responses to his behavior until I get to a point in our relationship where we can address (the causes of) his behavior in a more constructive way.	I'm going to give myself permission to let one thing go this month. I'm agreeing ahead of time that one thing will not be as perfect as I know that I can make it or as well thought out as it should be. The time I save here can buy me just a little bit of sanity.
How can I use these tools to change things? Because I'm being imaginative, I can assume that all of these things are, in some way, possible.	While doing the things above, I can also try to do the following:		
	Work on a protocol that allows all members of the grade team to get ideas and issues on the meeting agenda ahead of time, so more voices in the school can be heard.	Create better ways to respond to Marcus. The consequence-first way that we do discipline might work for some kids, but it does NOT work for Marcus. I can create structures that allow him to have more voice and autonomy, and I can try them out. This won't just be good for him; this can be good for lots of kids.	I can build a way for me to think about my work that allows me to prioritize tasks. There is too much to do. I cannot possibly do everything. I need to understand the things that I can afford to sidestep, and I can create a plan to communicate how and what I'll be working on instead, so that the people who depend on me understand my priorities.

How to Consume Professional Development Materials with Students in Mind

1 **Is this source credible? Whose work is the author referencing? Have I checked the original source?** Many of us won't go to a new hair salon without checking with five hundred other people who have used the same stylist, yet we follow the teaching advice that came up first on Google. When it's late on Sunday night, and the weekend has been great, and you just want *something* to teach tomorrow so that you can go to bed . . . you do a quick search online and run with the first result. We have all been there before. We must be more discerning in our research.

2 **In my experience, what parts of this ring true? What parts must I reconsider?** No credible advice or counsel is perfect. None. Just because a thing does not match your needs entirely does not mean that you must discount it. After receiving good counsel, you can build on it by considering your own experiences.

3 **If I were to try this tomorrow, what problems can I anticipate?** Nothing works perfectly the first time. When you try this new method, idea, text, or presentation, what problems will surface? Will all students find this accessible or engaging?

4 **How can I begin to solve those problems today?** What would you have to consider, include, change, or build?

5 **Who else is in this conversation?** Can you make yourself a steady diet of other educators, researchers, thought leaders, or colleagues who write, talk, blog, or tweet about this topic?

Figure 6.3 *How to Consume Professional Development Materials with Students in Mind*

directly impact my teaching and my ability to respond to kids." As I construct these goals, I'm holding on to the reality that Marcus' behavior will not change radically or immediately. I also know that the work will still be hard. Working toward a new reality for me, him, or any other kid will not ease my heartbreak. He will still make decisions that will challenge or frustrate me.

I can, however, expect to see small changes that, over time, will be huge for my relationship with Marcus and for my ability to deal productively with the Marcuses that I will encounter again in my career.

Because many are conditioned to look for the quick fix, I've also got to spend a bit of time teaching my colleagues, community members, and administrators how to see my work in ways that they can understand. I can do this by being clear about the actions that I intend to make and why I plan to make them. As you can see in Figure 6.4, that can sound any number of ways.

A blank Communication Plan (Online Resource 6.2) can be found with the Companion Resources.

Above all, what you communicate has to build realistic conditions for success. In teaching, sometimes I fear that we know how to communicate our work only in terms of miracles:

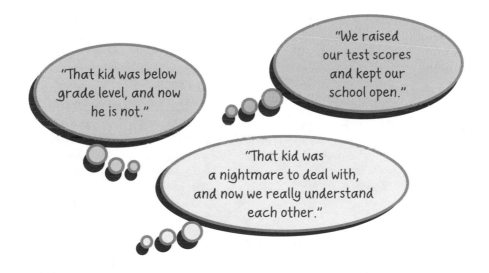

Figure 6.4 *Communication Plan*

What I Want to Do	How I Can Communicate My Plan	What That Might Sound Like
Because I know Marcus' patterns, I can create some go-to responses to his behavior until I get to a point in our relationship where we can address (the causes of) his behavior in a more constructive way.	I can show how this is tied to my students by using student work.	"When Marcus is off, the whole class is off. I'm building ways to respond to Marcus that are less confrontational to him and less disruptive to the class as a whole. By helping him to build the tools to govern himself, my goal is to get the class to twenty-five to thirty minutes of independent reading that are free of the procedural interruptions that happen when I have to govern Marcus."
While doing that, I can create better ways to respond to Marcus. The consequence-first way that we do discipline might work for some kids, but it does NOT work for Marcus. I can create structures that allow him to have more voice and autonomy, and I can try them out. This won't just be good for him; this can be good for lots of kids.	I can show how this action can make me and those around me better professionals.	"Working with Marcus in this way can help us to create opportunities for more students to feel like they have a place and a voice in the school. We'll have many more students like Marcus in the future, and we can all be more successful with an infrastructure that supports them more."
	I can talk about what this action will look like daily.	"This means that I'll be giving Marcus fewer office referrals and more opportunities to reflect and to work toward rebuilding the community and the relationships that are damaged by his actions."
My big fear is that I'll be on my own here—that I'll be seen as weak for not always leading with consequences.	I can talk about what those around me can expect to see in my classroom and in me. (And about what I can expect to see in myself.)	"At first this will feel a bit frustrating, because kicking Marcus out of class or out of school is easier. Keeping him in and working the community through Marcus' outbursts will be heavy emotional labor. That will be done through conversations, daily check-ins, and whole-class reflections at the end of each period."
	I can connect this action to a larger goal that the district or school wants to accomplish.	"If we are serious about reducing suspensions at the school, this can be a way. Perhaps we can use what we learn from working with Marcus to think about our schoolwide goals in a new way."

Again, we are slaves to the hero narrative. Though these realities exist, our day-to-day life feels more like this:

"The kids are stronger readers than they were when we started together. I've got the in-class data to show this, and the kids themselves can talk about their own learning. They went into that test confidently."

"That kid was below grade level and did not write anything at all. Now I'm getting a couple of sentences a day, and each day is a little bit better than the day before it."

"That kid is still hard to deal with, but we have created a system that allows all of us to learn in the ways that work best for us. Our days are not perfect, but we all feel respected and the class energy is focused on learning most of the time."

And we *must* find ways to be OK with that. Living in a reality that we articulate clearly and support with our own in-classroom data is one way to resist the notion that getting better at our jobs is prescriptively rote. Our work is constructive. As such it does not move forward if we wait for others to do all the building for us. We are not cogs that turn at the whim of student behavior, parental demands, or district mandates. Rather, we are architects that carefully consider how the experiences we design work optimally for the people that we serve. We cannot do this work without talking openly and acting boldly.

Feedback is an essential part of that design process.

It must start with us. So many times we look to others to articulate our value. If you are honest about what you see, no one can possibly know your worth and your toil like you.

There are three kinds of feedback that I consistently seek in school— mine, kids', and colleagues'. Most times I seek them in that order.

I like to think honestly about my own work first. After that, I seek counsel from children and colleagues.

It is hard to talk about another person's work without filtering it through the lens of one's own experience. Understanding this, I like to guide the feedback that I get by asking specific questions, like the ones in Figure 6.5. This ensures that the direction I get from my conversations with others reflects not just their autobiographical experience but the specific wisdom that they gleaned from that experience.

Figure 6.5 *Getting Feedback*

Mine	• What did I set out to do? • How much of it did I accomplish? • What adjustments do I need to make? • What plans do I need to make?
Kids'	• Over the last few days, name one thing that I did that really worked for you. • Name one thing that did not work at all. • If you could give me any advice that would make school better for you, what would it be?
Colleagues'	• Here is what I set out to do. . . . Here is what I did. . . . And here is how it went. . . . What do you see? You might notice things that I did not notice. • Here are the adjustments to my work that I'll be making moving forward. . . . Would you suggest anything else? • Here is how I have structured my plans, and here is what I plan to do. . . . Would you do anything else? Would you do anything differently?

Bring It Back to the Classroom

There is a sense of energy one feels after new professional learning—specifically when one feels like the newly acquired thing just might work, just might make a difference. This is the kind of energy that we carry into August after a particularly restful break or the vigor with which we leave good professional development or a productive chat with a trusted friend. This is that "I'mma walk in there and do what I do" energy. The "I don't care what they say; can't nobody stop me" energy. The energy that you don't even need a playlist for because it already has its own soundtrack in your mind. Wu-Tang.

This kind of energy burns bright, but sadly it also burns out, most often halting at signs of trouble.

As active practitioners, with complicated lives outside of school and teaching, it is so important to try what we learn. Immediately. If not, family and bills and small emergencies and random responsibilities start to accrue. Life happens, and nothing changes.

To combat this, I tell a friend and invite them to try the new thing with me.

> "Hey, I've been thinking lots about Marcus and his behavior patterns. I want to create better ways to respond to him. I'm going to try some new stuff on Tuesday. I'm not sure how it's going to go. Do you think that you can drop by during your prep for ten minutes just to watch me? I need somebody to have my back. Here is what you can expect to experience when you show up. . . ." Sometimes I even ask this of children.

Not only does this ensure my own safety, but it builds the foundation for a learning community that exists outside of the random prescriptions handed down from on high. Trying a new thing for the first time, I will make some missteps, but there will be another person—sometimes even a kid—who can keep me safe on the journey by providing feedback and support. We all need partners in the work—sidekicks even. Additionally, this allows me to try on the techniques and strategies that can most significantly impact my practice.

We can be public in our learning attempts. Sometimes we fear a thing because we might lose control of the kids if we try it and it does not work, so I include the kids in the work by explaining my attempt and how it will go and by soliciting their feedback. Sometimes we harbor similar fears of the adults in the building. "If someone finds out that I'm not good at this yet, they'll judge me," is such a profound deterrent to progress. I have found it helpful to talk openly about the things that I'm getting better at so that the attempt itself is unobstructed by the politics of school.

I have decided that I want to have better, more constructive responses to the children who need my urgent support in making better choices. I want to move away from punishment and shame into more demonstration and teaching. So that I can get to the work quickly, without fretting about all the different ways that things could go wrong, I name the work and start it right away—even when I know that my attempt will have some flaws. Again, what I am seeking here is the practice of teaching, not the perfection of it.

In this case, my work has three parts, as shown in Figure 6.6. First, I want to think, beforehand, about the common decisions that kids have to make in my class, and I want to consider the most common ways that those decisions can potentially derail learning. Beyond that I want to craft personal responses to each of those events, so that I will not be caught by surprise when kids choose to call out, leave their seats, or distract their peers.

I know that those things happen. Often. I want to be prepared for them.

A blank version of the Three-Part Plan for In-Classroom Work (Online Resource 6.3) can be found with the Companion Resources.

Once I craft responses, the second part of my work is to use them. Immediately.

Finally, my work ends at the end of class or at the end of the school day, when I reflect on how things went. Using questions like the ones in Figure 6.7, I ask myself what changed as a result of today's innovation. Was it the outcome that I expected to see? What would I need to do next to get closer to my expected outcome?

As I reflect, I try to keep an eye on student work. Did the new thing that I tried lead to more productive classroom conditions? Did that translate into actual productivity? Did the kids draw more, write more, do more math, or make more music?

I also like to think about their general affect. Was this a pleasant experience for the students?

A blank Reflection on Teaching Practice template (Online Resource 6.4) can be found with the Companion Resources.

The beauty in this reflective approach is that it's not just good for the specific work of responding to students' off-task decision making. It is good for our personal growth and our continued work as innovators. With some thought and some effort, we can make real change. We can be heroic.

Figure 6.6 *Three-Part Plan for In-Classroom Work*

Three-Part Plan for In-Classroom Work

Common Decisions Kids Have to Make in My Class	Am I going to get right to work when it's time or am I going to have a little chat (or a nice stroll around the room or an argument or a party)?	I don't understand. I'm not sure what's going on. What am I supposed to do next?
Ways Those Decisions Can Derail Learning	Practice is so essential to everything—math, reading, social studies, dance—and sometimes kids avoid practice. Especially when there exists an option to socialize with friends. Historically, my response tends to be a callout: "Marcus, get to your seat!" This is ineffective, even when it gets Marcus to move. It distracts the whole class, puts Daniel on the defensive, and leaves me vulnerable to a potential counteroffensive with a whole-class audience. I don't ever want to draw attention to off-task behavior, and that is exactly what callouts do.	For many kids, the only option they have is asking the teacher. Some do and get frustrated with the wait time it takes for me to get there. Others don't ask at all, and they decide to just chill or socialize.
Things That I Can Do	I can intercept Marcus if he's traversing the room and escort him back to his seat. Or I can ignore him for the time being, get everyone else settled, and then address the off-task behavior quietly. If most kids are invested, stopping class to address the three that aren't working yet, while risking the focus and attention of the thirty-two that are, just does not make mathematical sense. Additionally, if this is habitual behavior, Marcus and I can work out a nonverbal system of reminders that allow him to operate more independently, even when he finds himself off-task.	I can create systems where kids can talk to each other, and I can help them to practice using those systems responsibly. I can use visuals. Since kids are used to asking me, they won't use those visuals initially, but instead of answering their questions directly, I can redirect them to my visuals and we can answer their questions together.

Figure 6.7 *Reflection on Teaching Practice*

Reflection on Teaching Practice

What changed as a result of today's innovation?	
Was it the outcome I expected to see?	
What do I need to do next time to get closer to my expected outcome?	
Did today's innovation lead to more productive classroom conditions?	
Did today's innovation translate to productivity? How so?	
Was the experience pleasant for the students?	

Epilogue

The Gravity of Our Work

ALL THE TIME THAT I HAVE SPENT SKATEBOARDING HAS revealed several truths about my life. Specifically, it has revealed much about my life as an educator—about our shared work.

Among those truths, one of them continues to illuminate, even on my darkest days. It is this: Gravity comes for everyone.

No matter how we organize our escape from the surface of the earth, we are all brought back to meet it at the same rate of acceleration. We are siblings—bound not by blood, but by our shared attraction to the home that we share. More accurately, by its attraction to us.

Gravity—9.8 m/s^2—does not discriminate. What goes up, comes down. Fast. These are the rules.

As a skateboarder, I use wood, hard rubber, and momentum to live outside of those rules over and over again for whole afternoons at a time. And in this pursuit, I have learned that gravity comes for everyone except for those who use their creativity, their engineering, their resources, their tenacity, and their will to live outside of gravity's prescribed orthodoxy.

It is possible to take the parameters that we've been given and, within those parameters, create art that is both beautiful and proudly defiant.

This is what teaching must be. It cannot be orthodoxy that keeps us tethered to the earth. That has yielded what is—a savagely inequitable status quo.

We do not teach for what is. We teach for what can be.

The people that we admire most, no matter what their fields or disciplines, take the parameters that they have been given and create art. This act of radical creation is the only thing that can push those tired parameters into new paradigms. Not talk—us, doing the work.

Our tales of heroes and conquerors have created legends and deified the work. The problem with legends is that they are told in ways that exclude us. Progress is not the work of the gods or of a chosen elite. It is our work, and though it is hard, those who have made us believe that it is divine have orchestrated the most effective kind of oppression—one that takes our growth out of our hands and tasks it to those who "know better" than us.

Our way forward from here must recognize a new power: ours.

The work can be hard, but the steps are simple.

We set our goals, we learn, and we put that learning to use.

We stop regularly to reflect.

Knowing that big things don't change overnight, we take inventory of the small things that have changed. We name them and we celebrate them.

Then we make the necessary adjustments so that the work can continue. This will require effective study and teaching to drive us. This will require imagination to guide us. This will require love to keep us.

We got this.